LIVING VEDĀNTA

(VEDĀNTA CINTANAM)

Composition and Commentary
Swami Tejomayananda

Central Chinmaya Mission Trust

•

First Edition - August 2014 - 3000 copies
Reprint - January 2015 - 3000 copies

•

Published by:
Chinmaya Prakashan
The Publications Division of
Central Chinmaya Mission Trust
Sandeepany Sadhanalaya
Saki Vihar Road, Powai, Mumbai 400072, India
Tel.: +91-22-2857 2367, 2857 5806 Fax: +91-22-2857 3065
Email: ccmtpublications@chinmayamission.com
Website: www.chinmayamission.com

•

Distribution Centre in USA:
Chinmaya Mission West
Publications Division
560 Bridgetown Pike
Langhorne, PA 19053, USA
Tel.: 1-888-CMW-READ, (215) 396-0390 Fax: (215) 396-9710
Email: publications@chinmayamission.org
Website: www.chinmayapublications.org

•

Cover Photograph by
Asmani Kamat

•

Designed by:
Chinmaya Kalpanam, Mumbai

•

Printed by:
Usha Multigraphs Pvt. Ltd., Mumbai, India. Tel.: 24925354

•

Price: ₹ 65/-

•

ISBN 978-81-7597-643-6

CTP

Transliteration and Pronunciation Guide

In the book, Devanāgarī characters are transliterated according to the scheme adopted by the International Congress of Orientalists at Athens in 1912. In it one fixed pronunciation value is given to each letter; f, q, w, x and z are not called to use. An audio recording of this guide is available at http://chinmayamission.com/scriptures.php. According to this scheme:

Devanāgarī	Translit-eration	Sounds Like	Devanāgarī	Translit-eration	Sounds Like
अ	a	son	ढ्	ḍh	adhesive*
आ	ā	father	ण्	ṇ	under*
इ	i	different	त्	t	tabla
ई	ī	feel	थ्	th	thumb
उ	u	full	द्	d	this
ऊ	ū	boot	ध्	dh	Gandhi
ऋ	ṛ	rhythm*	न्	n	nose
ॠ	ṝ	**	प्	p	pen
ऌ	ḷ	**	फ्	ph	phantom*
ए	e	evade	ब्	b	boil
ऐ	ai	delight	भ्	bh	abhor
ओ	o	core	म्	m	mind
औ	au	now	य्	y	yes
क्	k	calm	र्	r	right
ख्	kh	khan	ल्	l	love
ग्	g	gate	व्	v	very
घ्	gh	ghost	श्	ś	shut
ङ्	ṅ	ankle*	ष्	ṣ	sugar
च्	c	chuckle	स्	s	simple
छ्	ch	witch*	ह्	h	happy
ज्	j	justice	ं	ṁ	improvise
झ्	jh	Jhansi	:	ḥ	**
ञ्	ñ	banyan	क्ष्	kṣ	action
ट्	ṭ	tank	त्र्	tr	three*
ठ्	ṭh	**	ज्ञ्	jñ	gnosis
ड्	ḍ	dog	ऽ	'	a silent 'a'

* These letters do not have an exact English equivalent. An approximation is given here.

** These sounds cannot be approximated in English words.

We take the opportunity to thank
Smt. Suneetha & Shri Umashankar Rajanahally, Davangere
for having sponsored the printing of this book
and ensuring that this timeless wisdom
reaches seekers all the world over.

Preface

Vedānta is the valid means that reveals the Truth. It makes us think about our relative relationship with the world and God and our essential nature.

The highlight of the annual Foundation Vedānta Course, popularly called the Dharma Sevak Course, is Pūjya Gurujī's visit and discourses. In 2013 during the end of the course, Pūjya Gurujī delivered discourses on *Living Vedānta* (*Vedānta Cintanam*). This empowered the 11th batch of Dharma Sevaks with practical ways of living Vedānta as they go back to the world of strife and tension.

Inspired by Pūjya Gurujī's discourses, the word meaning of the talks was given by Br. Anand, Brni. Darshika Chaitanya and her team of sevaks transcribed the talks. This was edited, formatted and printed by many more sevaks. Śrī Umashankar Rajanhally from Davangere, Karnataka, generously sponsored the first edition and also this reprint. May Pūjya Gurudev's blessings be on all.

Living Vedānta (*Vedānta Cintanam*) is Pūjya Gurujī's offerings to Śrī Rāma. May all partake of the prasāda of this offering.

Chinmaya Prakashan

Introduction

'Most problems would not arise, but for a moment's thought. But, a moment is a long time and thinking is a difficult process'. And we have neither a moment's time nor do we wish to do anything difficult ... But what is this life if full of care and we have no time to pause, think or stare – think about things which truly matter, think deeply about what is important in life. As most of our time is spent in the inconsequential, the routine or the urgent, we have no time left for the important things of life.

Cintanam is to think, reflect and ponder deeply. What should we reflect upon? Herein we shall think on the practical use of Vedānta in daily life.

What is Vedānta? Vedānta is the end portion of the Vedas also referred to as the Jñāna Kāṇḍa, the knowledge section of the Vedas. In fact it is the culmination of all knowledges, the ultimate knowledge contained in the Vedas. It is available as dialogues between the Guru and the disciple and these dialogues are also referred to as the Upaniṣads.

What is the function of Vedānta?

a. **Vedānta – a means of knowledge:** Vedānta is a means of knowledge to know oneself. Just as a mirror shows me myself (my body), Vedānta reveals my own true nature.

b. **Vedānta is knowledge of the Truth:** Vedānta is a unique knowledge wherein the knower becomes the known. Just as the dreamer awakens to become the waker, the finite knower ceases and realises his infinite nature.

c. **Vedānta is the proof of the Truth:** We always ask for proof, a way to verify what is told. The court asks for evidence and an intellectual asks for logic. With proof, belief becomes verified knowledge. Vedānta provides evidence and logic to verify Truth. Realisation of the Truth is the indisputable and uncontradictable evidence of the Truth.

The function of a means of knowledge is to reveal an object as it is (pramāyāḥ karaṇaṁ iti pramāṇam). It's job is not to create the object, but to bring it to our knowledge (jñāpakaṁ na tu kārakam). It removes the ignorance of the object and illumines it. For example, the sense of touch shows us that the nature of fire is heat and that it burns. It does not create the fire or the heat in the fire but only removes our ignorance about its hot nature.

Also the means of knowledge does not prompt us into action (na prerakam), but only reveals what can be done. What we do with the knowledge that is revealed is up to us. For example, I come to know that a cuddly rabbit or a deadly snake is in front of me. To fondle or run from the rabbit or the snake is left to me.

Vedānta introduces me to myself. Most in the world are either preparing to be happy or pretending to be happy. Vedānta puts an end to search for happiness as it reveals that I am the infinite source of all happiness. It ends my need to become something or someone as it makes me realise what I am already full and complete.

I was once asked a long time back, "What did Vedānta do for you? What did you get for the ten years of being in Chinmaya Mission and studying

Vedānta?" I said, "Before studying Vedānta, I would always ask – what will I get? – before doing anything. Now I have got something because of which this question has gone. My search has ended as I have found what I was searching for."

So why should I know Vedānta? If I am working for a company, I should know my designation in the company, my place of work, the working of the company and also who my boss and the owner of the company is. Then alone will I fit into the company, relate to all appropriately and work to satisfy the boss, progress personally and achieve my company's goals. When we know the nature of things we can make use of them beneficially. For example, I cook food and enjoy a hot meal because I know that fire heats.

Vedānta teaches us about who we are, what is the nature of the world and the big boss of the world – God. When we know our transactional and absolute relation with all beings, the world and God, we will be able to relate and interact appropriately and successfully.

Śrī Ramana Maharshi says, 'Without knowing the knower, can our knowledge be considered valid or real?'[1] It would be quite frightening if we forget who we are and our near and dear ones.

Two elderly ladies went for a drive. Concerned by her driving, her friend said, "Do you know you jumped through three red lights?" The friend exclaimed, "O dear, am I driving?" Such 'senior moments' can be quite disastrous. We get enslaved by objects, attached to our body, stressed at our work place, have problems in our relationships, are unhappy with our relatives, get scared of challenges and become bored with life.

Vedānta teaches us about the nature of the individual, the world and the Lord. *Vedānta Cintanam* guides us how we can apply this knowledge in our life. A doctor who cannot diagnose and treat the patient is not considered a good doctor, even if he has a lot of knowledge of medicine. Of what use is the knowledge if it does not translate into practical usage. *Vedānta Cintanam* teaches us how to intelligently translate the knowledge gained through the Guru and the scriptures into right vision and action. For example, Vedānta says that I am not the body. Now,

[1] *boddhāram-ātmānam-ajānato yo bodhaḥ sa kiṁ syāt paramārthabodhaḥ*
– *Saddarśana*-13

how should I look upon it? This guidance applies for those who have at least heard and understood Vedānta intellectually (parokṣa jñāna).

The question of guidance and application of the knowledge of Vedānta does not arise for one who has directly realised (aparokṣa jñāna) the truth of Vedānta. He is then seen to be choicelessly living Vedānta.

The first verse is an invocation prayer and it also introduces the theme of the text.

श्रीरामाय नमस्तुभ्यं कृपया तव शक्यते ।
सुखेनाभ्यसितुं लब्धं ज्ञानं दैनिकजीवने ॥ १ ॥

śrīrāmāya namastubhyaṁ kṛpayā tava śakyate,
sukhenābhyasituṁ labdhaṁ jñānaṁ dainika-jīvane. (1)

श्रीरामाय – to Śrī Rāma; नमः – salutations; तुभ्यम् – to You; तव कृपया – by Your grace; शक्यते – it is possible; सुखेन – with ease; अभ्यसितुम् – to practise; लब्धम् – attained; ज्ञानम् –knowledge; दैनिकजीवने – in daily life

1. Salutations to Lord Śrī Rāma! It is by Thy grace alone one is able to practise the gained knowledge with ease in one's daily life.

Salutations again and again to Lord Śrī Rāma. It is only by Your grace that I compose these verses and explain them. Your grace alone enables me to understand Vedānta and live the knowledge easily.

It is difficult to carry a big and heavy bag. But a bag with wheels can be dragged quite easily, even by a child. Similarly a difficult task becomes easy to accomplish with the grace of God.

It is difficult to understand the deep import of Vedānta and even more difficult to live this knowledge. We find ourselves confused and confounded on many occasions. Despite our understanding our attachments, prejudices and the like, make it difficult to deal with our mind and the world. This becomes easy with the grace of God.[1]

[1] *durgama kāja jagat ke jete, sugama anugraha tumhare tete – 20*
– Hanumāna Cālīsā

The next verse expounds the glory of Vedānta.

वेदान्तदर्शनं शुद्धं प्रत्यक्षानुभवं परम् ।
सर्वदा येऽनुतिष्ठन्ति प्राप्यते तैर्ध्रुवं पदम् ॥ २ ॥

vedānta-darśanaṁ śuddhaṁ pratyakṣānubhavaṁ param,
sarvadā ye'nutiṣṭhanti prāpyate tair-dhruvaṁ padam. (2)

वेदान्तदर्शनम् – the vision of Vedānta; **शुद्धम्** – sacred/ purifying; **प्रत्यक्ष-अनुभवम्** – is directly experienced; **परम्** – supreme; **सर्वदा** – at all times; **ये** – they who; **अनुतिष्ठन्ति** – remain steadfast (in it); **प्राप्यते** – is attained; **तैः** – by them; **ध्रुवं पदम्** – the eternal goal

2. The vision of Vedānta is supreme, sacred, purifying and can be directly experienced. Those who remain steadfast in it, they attain the eternal goal.

Vedānta Darśana – the Vision of Vedānta: As the vision so the world appears to us (yathā dṛṣṭi tathā sṛṣṭi). Vedānta gives us the right vision of looking at ourselves, the world of things and beings and the Lord. It explains the relative and absolute nature of everything.

Pure and Purifying (śuddham): There are many products that cleanse our body and purify the water and refresh the air. Water and fire are natural purifiers. Mantras purify and sanctify the atmosphere and our speech and a dip in the holy river cleanses our sins. But these have a short or long term effect. Self-knowledge removes our wrong notions and ignorance and cleanses us whole and complete, once and for all. That is why it is said that there is no greater purifier than Self-knowledge.[1]

Supreme (param): Vedānta is the knowledge of the supreme Truth and also the highest knowledge as it puts an end to our sorrow and seeking. It is the very foundation of all knowledges.[2]

Directly experienced (pratyakṣa-anubhavam): Heaven can be directly experienced only when one dies and has enough merits to go there. Most scientific facts are only heard or read truths for which we have neither the equipment, time or ability to verify directly. However the knowledge of Vedānta can be experienced and verified directly by anyone who has a pure mind.

---

[1] *na hi jñānena sadṛśaṁ pavitram-iha vidyate – Gītā*-4.38

[2] *sarva-vidyā-pratiṣṭhām – Muṇḍaka Upaniṣad*-1.1

This knowledge can be attained by anyone irrespective of their caste, creed, colour, gender, nationality or religion. Even an illiterate person can gain the supreme Truth. The great lineage of saints through the ages are a proof to the universal nature of the knowledge of Vedānta.

Eternal Goal (dhruvaṁ padam): In this world conditioned by time, the Truth alone is eternal. Those who pursue the eternal Truth with consistent efforts themselves become immortal – unconditioned by time.

What does Vedānta say?

नाहङ्कारो मनोबुद्धिर्देहो नाहं कदाचन ।
इति वेदान्तवाक्यस्य भावश्चिन्त्यः पुनः पुनः ॥ ३ ॥

nāhaṅkāro mano-buddhir-deho nāhaṁ kadācana,
iti vedānta-vākyasya bhāvaścintyaḥ punaḥ punaḥ. (3)

न – not; अहङ्कारः – the ego; मनः – mind; बुद्धिः – intellect; देहः – body; अहम् – I; न कदाचन – (am) never; इति – thus; वेदान्तवाक्यस्य भावः – the import of the Vedāntika statement; चिन्त्यः – one should ponder over; पुनः पुनः – again and again

3. 'I am never the ego, mind, intellect and body.' One should ponder over the import of this Vedāntika statement again and again.

The knower is different from the known: I see the pot, but I do not become the pot. I remain different from the pot. Similarly I perceive my body, know my mind, and intellect, and experience the presence and absence of the ego in the waking and the deep sleep state. Hence I am not the body, mind, intellect or the ego (I-notion).

The body is known. It can be repaired and its parts replaced. Some outsource their heart or liver, some transplant their hair or implant their teeth. A convict in jail first got his tonsils, and teeth removed. Then, he got one kidney and his appendix removed. The warden suspected that he was planning his escape in stages!

Vedānta helps us ascertain that we are not the body-mind-intellect. This is a powerful knowledge. In fact it is quite mind-blowing and contradictory to our usual belief and the knowledge of most in the world.

Will this knowledge harm my personal, social or professional life? Do I have to neglect or destroy my body? How then should I relate to those related to my body like my family and friends. What should I call myself? Does this mean that our body does not exist? The answer to such questions is given in the following verses.

How can we deny the existence of the body we so evidently experience and because of which alone we experience this world and read this book? It is explained thus –

तेषामात्मत्वमात्रं हि निरस्तमिह नास्तिता ।
योजनीयाश्च तस्मात्ते व्यवहारे विवेकतः ॥ ४ ॥

teṣām-ātmatva-mātraṁ hi nirastam-iha nāstitā,
yojanīyāśca tasmāt-te vyavahāre vivekataḥ. (4)

तेषाम् – of them (of these four factors); आत्मत्वमात्रम् – the Selfhood (assumption of them to be self); हि – alone; निरस्तम् – is negated; इह – here; न – not; अस्तिता – (their) existence; योजनीयाः – should be employed; च – and; तस्मात् – therefore; ते – they; व्यवहारे – in daily life; विवेकतः – with discrimination

4. Here (in the above statement) the Selfhood of them (the factors mentioned) alone is negated and not their existence. Therefore they should be used thoughtfully in daily life.

Existence of body and bodily existence: The knowledge, 'I am not the body', does not deny or negate the existence of the body. Not only is the body experienced, but it remains as the counter of the experiences of the world. However it is now experienced as 'mine' and not as 'I'.

The individual lives as the body from birth to death. He identifies with it and assumes the characteristics of the body as his thinking that 'I am fair and slim' or 'I am dark and handsome'. This 'I' notion (Selfhood) in the body is negated with the knowledge, 'I am not the body'.

One who knows, 'I am not the body', experiences the body and experiences through the body and one who knows not, has bodily experiences. One lives in the body, the other as the body.

Intelligent use of the body: The proud owner of an expensive car takes good care of it and maximises its use. He reads all instructions and trains to drive it well.

I once blew out a new radio that I plugged into a 220 volt connection instead of the 6 volts, as written in the book of instruction. No use of blaming the radio or the plug point. I should have known better! The scriptures give us instructions of how to use the body intelligently, so that we can accomplish our goals and be happy.

Disuse of the body: Some are lazy and do not use their body. Like a clean and polished car, always kept in a garage, some dress well, put on make-up and just adorn their homes with their presence. A lazy person was enjoying a book titled, 'Meditation for Those Who Do Nothing, and Want to Do Even Less'. Laziness is a great enemy of man.[1]

Abuse of the body: Some pamper and indulge the body and cater to its every desire and craving. Some abuse it with heavy drinking, smoking or drugs. A man enslaved by pleasures is unable to give them up even when they cause disease and death.[2]

Underutilisation of the body: A proud possessor of a smart phone may not be smart enough to use

[1] *ālasya hi manuṣyasya śarīrasya mahāripuḥ – Subhāṣita*

[2] *sukhataḥ kriyate rāmābhogaḥ paścāt-hanta śarīre rogaḥ,*
yadyapi loke maraṇaṁ śaraṇaṁ tadapi na muñcati pāpācaraṇam
– Bhaja Govindam-28

most of its apps. He uses it like any other ordinary phone. Most are unaware of the special features of this most sophisticated human body and use it like any other body of any other living being, just to exist and survive.

Overuse of the body: An overworked machine breaks down easily. The overworked jet-setting executive gets peptic ulcers at twenty-five and a fatal heart attack at thirty!

What then is the intelligent use of the body?

नरदेहः पुण्यप्राप्तः सर्वभूतहिते सदा ।
निःश्रेयसि च योक्तव्यः सर्वेशे चातिप्रेमतः ॥ ५ ॥

nara-dehaḥ puṇya-prāptaḥ sarvabhūta-hite sadā,
niḥśreyasi ca yoktavyaḥ sarveśe cātipremataḥ. (5)

नरदेहः – the human body; पुण्यप्राप्तः – attained by one's merits; सर्वभूतहिते – in the welfare of all beings; सदा – always; निःश्रेयसि – in attaining Liberation; च – and; योक्तव्यः – should be employed; सर्वेशे – in the supreme Lord of all; च – and; अतिप्रेमतः – with extreme love and devotion

5. Human body is gained as a result of countless merits. It should always be employed in the welfare of all beings, in attaining Liberation and in supreme devotion to God.

A Rare Gift: Human life is special, unique, rare and therefore precious. It is attained due to the merits of many lifetimes and through the grace of God.[1] The human birth is indeed the rarest of births.[2] Herein we are bestowed with choice – the freedom to do, not to do or do otherwise[3] – indeed a great boon. We can thereby make or mar our life.

The dignity of human life is in being humane. We can also become divine. This is not possible in any other body. If we do not attain divinity it is indeed a big mistake, a lost opportunity and a great loss.[4]

What should we do with this special body and mind? This body indeed is the first vehicle for doing dharma.[5] We should use it –

a. **For the welfare of all beings (sarva-bhūta-hite):** Most people live a self-centered life, caring little for other human beings, leave alone thinking of the welfare of other living beings. Plants and

---

1 *durlabhaṁ trayam-evaitad-devānugraha-hetukaṁ,*
manuṣyatvaṁ mumukṣutvaṁ mahāpuruṣa-saṁśrayaḥ
– *Vivekacūḍāmaṇi*-3

2 *jantūnāṁ nara-janma durlabham – Vivekacūḍāmaṇi*-2

3 *kartuṁ śakyaṁ, akartuṁ śakyam, anyathā kartuṁ śakyam*

4 *iha ced-avedīt-atha satyam-asti na ced-ihāvedīt-mahatī vinaṣṭiḥ*
– *Kena Upaniṣad*-2.5

5 *śarīram-ādyaṁ khalu dharma-sādhanam*

animals can live without us, but we cannot live without them. We are the big brothers of this earth family and it is our duty and responsibility to take care of other beings, the environment and live in harmony with all. We should not harm others for our pleasure or progress.

Some make it their life's mission to protect trees (Chipko Movement), some to protect rivers (Save Ganga Movement), some to take care of animals (PETA), some for world peace, some for the freedom of the country, some to protect women and children and some to discover the truths of nature or cure of diseases. To work selflessly for the sake of others, for noble goals, without likes and dislikes, with love and dedication, is called Karma Yoga.

b. **For attaining Liberation (niḥśreyasa):** Human birth is special because it is the doorway to Liberation. We strive for great name, fame, power, position, wealth, pleasure, adulation and following for becoming happy. Liberation is attainment of unconditioned Bliss, freedom from sorrow, stress and limitations and freedom from the cycle of birth and death. Gain of finite name, fame and so on is fine, but the gain of infinitude is the highest goal of human life (parama puruṣārtha). I have seen sparrows pecking at the mirror, trying to meet the sparrow reflected in the mirror. Even when the mirror is covered, they in ignorance come again and again. Alas they have no Guru or scripture to point out that they are seeking only themselves. To pursue the path of knowledge in order to know one's own true nature and to gain Liberation is called Jñāna Yoga.

c. **For devotion to God (sarveśe atipremataḥ):** Love unites. Love for the omniscient, omnipotent, omnipresent Lord, who is creator, nourisher and protector of all and the very indwelling Self in all, unites us with the entire universe. Animals too have love but cannot love God or love all as God, nor create such love in the hearts of all. This is the speciality of human birth. To cultivate supreme love for the Supreme is called Bhakti Yoga.

The human body is the result of meritorious deeds of past lives. The result of actions, good or bad, from the past and present life come to us in the present as external circumstances and the condition of the body and mind. How should we deal with them, knowing that 'I am not the body'?

अनिष्टमिष्टं मिश्रं च फलं प्राप्नोति मानवः ।
कृतकर्मानुसारेण समत्वं तेषु धारयेत् ॥ ६ ॥

aniṣṭam-iṣṭaṁ miśraṁ ca phalaṁ prāpnoti mānavaḥ,
kṛta-karmānusāreṇa samatvaṁ teṣu dhārayet. (6)

अनिष्टम् – undesired; इष्टम् – desired; च – and; मिश्रम् – mixed; फलम् – result; प्राप्नोति – attains; मानवः – human being; कृत-कर्म-अनुसारेण – as per the acts done; समत्वम् – equanimity; तेषु – in them (the results); धारयेत् – should maintain

6. Bad (undesired/sorrowful), good (desired/joyful), and mixed results are caused by man's (own) karmas. He should maintain equanimity in them.

Results of actions can be categorised into three types depending on how we look upon them.

1. **Undesired Results (aniṣṭam):** Results which we call unconducive or bad. I put my money in a bank that goes bankrupt. My son-in-law gets fired from his job. I develop a lump in my stomach, however benign it may be. A man asked his Guru, "Why are problems coming to me one after another?" The Guru said, "Thank God they are coming one after another and not simultaneously!" Sometimes what we term undesired may actually in the long run be good for us. Steve Jobs was kicked out of Apple and he started a new company, was rehired by his old company and attained greater fame.

2. **Desired Results (iṣṭam):** Results which we call conducive or good. Winning a lottery, children who obey their parents, getting miraculously saved in an accident are considered good results or the blessings of God.

However something that looks good today may lead to undesired consequences like wealth creating conflicts between family members.

3. **Mixed Results (miśram):** Results which are neither good nor bad, or both. Average marks in a test paper, a promotion that brings more pay and longer work hours or the robber steals the diamond ring but overlooks the diamond necklace. Such results cause neither joy nor sorrow or both together. When we get good and bad news together we do not know whether to laugh or cry!

As we sow, so we reap: Getting the result of actions is not a choice. Once we have done something, the results shall come, in their own destined time, in their own destined way. Whatever be the nature of the results, we should remember that they are the results of our own actions. We cannot blame anyone for what we get. We may not remember what we have done and wonder 'why me?' or 'what have I done to deserve this?'... Whether we accept it or not, we deserve what we get. When I feel sick, I may not remember what I ate, but the body remembers and responds by throwing up.

What should be my attitude in facing these results?

Keep cool and respond (samatvam): As we face challenges which are only the results of our actions, we must first and foremost be alert, keep cool and not react. A reactive and agitated mind is unable to deal with the situation. A man was told that his godown has got burnt. He said 'What?' and then said 'So what!'

A man lost all his money in Las Vegas. He then bet mentally and lost his mind! Overjoyed another man threw a lavish party when he was told that he had won a lottery. The next day he came to know it was a mistake, he had not won it! The highs and lows of life should be faced with equanimity.

Also we should not act when the mind is reacting and agitated. Only when the mind is calm can we respond appropriately to the situation.

Vedānta says 'I am not the mind.' How should I translate this knowledge in my life?

यस्माद्दते न किञ्चन क्रियते कर्म मानवैः।
तन्मनः कल्पनारूपं योज्यतां सावधानतः ॥ ७ ॥

yasmād-ṛte na kiñcana kriyate karma mānavaiḥ,
tanmanaḥ kalpanā-rūpaṁ yojyatāṁ sāvadhānataḥ. (7)

यस्मात् ऋते – without which (in the absence of which); न – not; किञ्चन – even a little; क्रियते – is done; कर्म – action; मानवैः – by men; तत् – that; मनः – mind; कल्पनारूपम् – of the nature of thoughts/imagination; योज्यताम् – should be used; सावधानतः – with caution

7. That without which men cannot perform any action is the mind which is of the form of thoughts. It should be used with great caution.

What is the mind?

a. **Mind – instrument of thinking:** The faculty of thinking is called the mind (manute anena iti manaḥ).

b. **Mind – a flow of thoughts:** It is a continuous flow of thoughts of varied kinds like desire, will, intention, imagination, ideas ... (kalpanā-rūpa, vṛtti-pravāha-rūpa).

c. **Mind – the instrument of experiences:** The body is the counter through which we transact with the world (bhogāyatana) and the mind is the instrument of all our experiences (bhoga-sādhana) – good or bad, joyful or sorrowful.

d. **Mind – the doer of all actions:** It is the mind alone that does all the actions. When the mind is dormant as in deep sleep, we cannot do any conscious action or interaction. The body is only the tool that the mind employs to accomplish its tasks. The body never acts on its own and therefore a man in coma cannot do anything. The body is like the hardware and the mind like the software because of which the computer works. When the software gets infected with viruses it can cause a lot of problems and even crash. How should we deal with the mind?

The mind is the most sophisticated and delicate instrument. It should therefore be used with great care and caution. It is therefore important to learn how to think and what to think.

Should we fight the storms of the mind or escape from its vagaries? The following verse teaches us how to befriend our mind.

विषयासक्तिरूपेण मनो बन्धनकारकम् ।
ईश्वरार्पितरूपेण तन्मनो मुक्तिसाधकम् ॥ ८ ॥

viṣayāsakti-rūpeṇa mano bandhana-kārakam,
īśvarārpita-rūpeṇa tanmano mukti-sādhakam. (8)

विषयासक्तिरूपेण – in the form of having attachment to objects; मनः – mind; बन्धन-कारकम् – is the creator/cause of bondage; ईश्वरार्पितरूपेण – as absorbed or offered to God; तत् – that; मनः – mind; मुक्ति-साधकम् – helps attain Liberation

8. Mind attached to sense objects causes bondage. Absorbed in God or offered to God, the same mind leads one to Liberation.

Why do we fight the mind? 'Because it is troubling me.' Why does the mind trouble? What does it want? It is better to understand the mind than fight a loosing battle with it.

The mind is always in search of happiness. It wants to be happy. It goes with the senses into the world of objects to be happy. Dancers are instructed that the eyes should go where the hand goes and the mind should go where the eyes go.[1] Our mind along with the senses enjoys the dancer's movements, the magician's tricks, the TV shows or the window shopping.

But do the objects of the world really have happiness? If it were so, like sweetness in sugar, they would give the same degree of happiness to all, at all times. But no thing, being or circumstance is able to do so. In fact we experience the law of diminishing returns at work and most things that we imagine are joy-giving, turn out to be disappointments and at times disasters.

What actually happens when we enjoy objects. With a desire in the mind for happiness we contact the objects through our senses. The mind temporarily becomes calm when the desire is fulfilled, which results in the manifestation of the happiness within. Not knowing that the joy experienced is from within, we superimpose it on the object and feel that the object

[1] *yato hasta tato dṛṣṭiḥ yato dṛṣṭi tato manaḥ*

has made me happy. We therefore become attached to objects and beings.

Some are attached to gross objects like food, others pursue subtler joys of literature and yet others enjoy through still subtler pursuits like meditation – all with the false notion that they are joy-giving. The more the joy superimposed, the greater is the attachment. Attachment causes dependence, possessiveness, jealousies, fear and so on. These naturally cause sorrow, tension and agitation. Dependence on things, beings, feelings or circumstances, itself is sorrow.[1] We then feel that we cannot live without the objects. Having imagined happiness in objects, man gets bound to them by the rope of attachment like an animal (leashed to a post). When the false notion goes, the mind becomes detached and free.[2]

So how can we free our mind from its attachments? We hold on to our childhood toys as

[1] *sarvaṁ paravaśaṁ duḥkham*

[2] *dehādi-sarva-viṣaye parikalpya rāgaṁ*
badhnāti tena puruṣaṁ paśuvat guṇena,
vairasyamatra viṣavat-suvidhāya paścāt
enaṁ vimocayati tanmana eva bandhāt – Vivekacūḍāmaṇi-173

long as we thought they were fun. But we outgrew our attachments to one toy effortlessly when we thought it had no fun value or when we found another which was more fun. It is difficult to get rid of all our attachments and impossible to unhook the mind from objects without giving it another source of happiness as the mind cannot remain without holding on to something. The pleasure seeking mind should be turned towards the true source of joy – the Lord.

The mind usually pursues objects because of its likes and dislikes. When it is dedicated to God all actions are performed without likes and dislikes and as an offering to God, in the same way as a man dedicated to his company works sincerely without likes and dislikes during office time only for the sake of the company and to please the boss. Such a worshipful attitude invokes the grace of God which in turn purifies the mind just as the boss, pleased with the sincerity and hard work of his employee promotes him.

Thus choiceless performance of one's duties as worship of God frees the mind from selfishness and attachments and such a pure mind is then fit for Liberation. Many seekers have reported that as their love for satsaṅga, study of the scriptures and spiritual practices has increased, their attachment to partying, socialising, shopping or watching TV has decreased. Old attachments loose hold on us and the mind is then available for higher pursuits.

When the mind becomes pure, steady and subtle, it turns within to the true source of joy, becomes absorbed in God, thereafter the Truth reveals itself and the person is liberated. Thus a mind full of attachments leads to sorrow and bondage and a mind absorbed in God leads to peace and fulfilment.

Therefore –

तस्मात्सदा हि ध्यातव्यं साधकेन प्रयत्नतः।
मनो मे शिवसङ्कल्पमस्तु ते कृपया प्रभो॥ ९॥

tasmāt-sadā hi dhyātavyaṁ sādhakena prayatnataḥ,
mano me śiva-saṅkalpam-astu te kṛpayā prabho. (9)

तस्मात् – therefore; सदा – always; हि – indeed; ध्यातव्यं – should be contemplated; साधकेन – by a seeker; प्रयत्नतः – with lot of effort; मे – my; मनः – mind; शिव-सङ्कल्पम्-अस्तु – be of auspicious thoughts alone; ते कृपया – by Your grace; प्रभो – O Lord!

9. Therefore a spiritual seeker should always pray thus: 'O Lord! through Your grace may my mind be filled with auspicious thoughts.'

I am not the mind, but I have to live with the mind, morning to night, birth to death. So instead of cursing and complaining, it should be guided with all alertness and efforts towards God.

Each time that the child tries to dash out of the door, the mother carefully pulls him back from a potential accident. Her mind is ever alert and quick to respond, however fast the child runs. Similarly we too have to practise 'mindful living' or 'conscious living' and not allow the mind to get attached or entertain wrong notions. It is difficult to do so constantly so we resort to a higher source for help.

Prayer to God – mano me śiva-saṅkalpam-astu

a. **May my mind have auspicious thoughts:** O Lord, You are omnipotent and omniscient. By Your grace anything and everything is possible. May my mind entertain auspicious thoughts. May my mind be filled with faith, devotion, discrimination, dispassion, good intentions and so on.

b. **May my mind seek God (Śiva):** Instead of running after worldly objects, may my mind desire to see His form, hear His stories, know Him, meet Him and become one with Him.

c. **May His will become mine:** Everything happens by God's will. May I have no will or wish other than His, may His will become my will. May I always surrender to His will. May His will alone prevail as I know that it will be for my good and will bring me close to Him. Initially Arjuna was unwilling to listen to the Lord Śrī Kṛṣṇa's command to fight. After hearing the knowledge of the *Gītā,* wisdom dawned and he says, "I shall do as You say".[1]

We thus realise that the mind which broods over worldly objects, gets attached to them and the mind that entertains auspicious thoughts and remembers God, gets absorbed in God.[2]

---

[1] *kariṣye vacanaṁ tava – Gītā*-18.73

[2] *viṣayān dhyāyata cittaṁ viṣayeṣu viṣajjate,*
mām-anusmarataścittaṁ mayyeva pravilīyate

Vedānta says that I am not the intellect which is subtler than the mind. How should I translate this in my daily life?

बुद्धिं तु सारथिं विद्धि या नयेद्रथजीवनम् ।
कार्याकार्यविवेकेन मनुष्यस्य दिने दिने ॥ १० ॥

buddhiṁ tu sārathiṁ viddhi yā nayed-ratha-jīvanam,
kāryākārya-vivekena manuṣyasya dine dine. (10)

बुद्धिम् – the intellect; तु – also; सारथिम् – the charioteer; विद्धि – know; या – which; नयेत् – pulls/leads; रथजीवनम् – chariot of life; कार्य-अकार्य-विवेकेन – by distinguishing between what should be done and what should not be done; मनुष्यस्य – of man; दिने दिने – day after day

10. Know the intellect to be the charioteer of man's chariot of life that leads it day by day through understanding of karmas to be done and to be avoided.

What is the intellect? The intellect is subtler than the mind and a very powerful instrument that leads our life. Like the mind it also constitutes of thoughts.

The mind is a seat of emotions like love, compassion, anger, greed and so on. The intellect has thoughts like observation, understanding, creativity and so on.

How does it function? The senses perceive the various sense objects. The eyes see colour and form, the ears hear sounds and so on. These inputs from the senses are carried by the mind, collated and put before the intellect. The intellect analyses, understands and decides what to do. Its decisions are carried out by the mind through sense organs of action and the body. For example, I see and hear my friend narrate a joke. I understand it and respond with laughter. I step on a burning cigarette and immediately lift my foot and cry out in pain as commanded by the intellect.

Much like the doctor analyses, diagnoses and prescribes the medicines based on the pathologist's reports or the executive decides the policies of the company based on the reports of each department, the intellect decides, based on the data provided by the mind, the senses and past experiences or memory.

What is its role? With the mind as the reins of the horses of the senses, the intellect is like the driver of the chariot of our life. If the horses are untamed and the driver lets loose the reins, the owner is in trouble. A man seen clinging to the neck of a fast galloping horse was asked by a passer-by, where he was going. He replied, 'Don't ask me. Ask the horse!' However if the horses are well trained and the driver has control over the reins and the horses, the owner has a comfortable ride and soon reaches his goal. The intellect is the driver that takes us to our goal.

The intellect helps us to decide the course of action we must take each moment as we go through life. It guides us in ordinary matters like what to order in a restaurant, to more serious matters like what to study, which job offer to accept and whom to marry. It can decide even subtler matters like what is my duty, what is right and wrong (ethical and unethical), what I should do and not do and what leads to bondage and what will liberate.[1]

The highest use of intellect is in determining what is the Self and not-Self (ātma-anātma viveka), the eternal and the ephemeral (nitya-anitya viveka) or the real and the unreal (sad-asad viveka). The

---

[1] *pravṛttiṁ ca nivṛttiṁ ca kāryākārye bhayābhaye,*
bandhaṁ mokṣaṁ ca yā vetti buddhiḥ sā pārtha sāttvikī.

– *Gītā*-18.30

best decision that the intellect can take is to seek the Infinite/God, surrender the body-mind-intellect to Him, serve Him and live by His will. Animals too have an intellect that they effectively employ in ordinary matters like what to eat, but they do not have the privilege to determine higher matters and they cannot decide to surrender their intellect. Arjuna was unable to decide what should be done in the Mahābhārata war. He was confused because of his attachment to his teacher and grandsire. Lord Śrī Kṛṣṇa, his charioteer, guided him to take the right course of action which when he followed, resulted in victory.

How should we use the intellect? On what basis should it determine the nature of things and decide on the course of action?

यद्विषये प्रमाणं यज्जानीयात् तत्प्रमाणतः ।
स्वरूपं निश्चितं तस्य कर्म कुर्यान्नरस्ततः ॥ ११ ॥

yadviṣaye pramāṇaṁ yajjānīyāt tatpramāṇataḥ,
svarūpaṁ niścitaṁ tasya karma kuryānnarastataḥ. (11)

यद् विषये – in any object; प्रमाणम् – valid means of knowledge; यत् – whichever (is appropriate); जानीयात् – should know; तत् – by; प्रमाणतः – (by that) means; स्वरूपम् – essential nature; निश्चितम् – certainly; तस्य – its; कर्म – action; कुर्यात् – should perform; नरः – man; ततः – thereafter

11. Man should know with certainty the nature of a given thing with the valid means of knowledge appropriate for that object or field. Thereafter he should perform the action.

The intellect is the faculty of knowing and verifying what is known. Knowledge and verification is possible only with the right means of knowledge. For hearing sounds, ears are the means of knowledge and not the eyes. The eyes can see the radio and determine by a light that it is working, but cannot hear the music, even if we stare at it for a long time. We can feel food with our hand and infer that it must be delicious by the look and fragrance, but its tastiness can only be verified by the tongue.

The story of the blind men and the elephant is famous. Each felt one limb of the elephant and concluded it was a pillar (leg), a broom (tail) and a hose pipe (trunk). Even when their perceptions were put together, they could not figure out that it was an elephant as they did not have right means to know and verify.

The study of the various means of knowledge (pramāṇa vicāra) forms a basic and important part of the study of Vedānta. Interestingly, Epistemology termed Theory of Knowledge (TOK) is an important and compulsory subject in the popular IB (International Baccalaureate) curriculum, wherein they discuss 'how we know what we know' through the study of various means of knowledge and areas of knowledge.

There are many means of knowledge. The three main ones are:

1. **Direct perception (pratyakṣa pramāṇa):** It is the fundamental means without which no knowledge can take place. All other means are based on perception. The sense organs of seeing (eyes), hearing (ears), tasting (tongue), touching (skin) and smelling (nose) give us the knowledge of colour and form, sounds, tastes, feelings and smell (rūpa, śabda, rasa, sparśa and gandha).

2. **Inference (anumāna pramāṇa):** Inference uses direct perception and logic to know. When I see that the roads are wet in the morning, I infer that it must have rained at night, even though I did not directly see the rains. My previously gained knowledge that whenever it rains, the roads get wet is the basis for my inference. Ramesh does not eat all day, yet he is fat, so he must be eating at night. A man went to a government office to meet the officer. He was told by the peon, by the orders of the officer, that the officer was absent. Despite that he waited, till the officer finally called him in and asked him, "Why did you wait, when you were told I was not there?" The man said, "I knew

you were in the office, as all the staff in your outer office were at their desk, working. In your absence they would have gone for a tea break or would be chit-chatting." Such and many other things are determined by the intellect through inference.

3. **Verbal testimony (śabda pramāṇa):** It is based on direct perception and authority of the written and spoken word. I watch the on site report of the Ganesh festivities on the TV and know about what is happening in Mumbai. Most of our knowledge of the world comes from newspapers, TV, books, google, pictures and narration by others who may or may not have directly experienced the knowledge. Most scientific facts are known through the authority of the teacher and books, who themselves have based their knowledge on other teachers and books. We know about heaven and hell through the scriptures.

Faith in the means of knowledge is needed for any knowledge and therefore it is said that one with faith, knows.[1] We need to have faith that my eyes see correctly, or that my logic is right or the teacher who teaches knows the subject or that the scriptures speak the truth.

[1] *śraddhāvān-labhate jñānam – Gītā*-4.39

Knowing, verifying and deciding what to do: Knowledge should be acquired through the right means of knowledge. The intellect should understand what is the right means. Thereafter it has to be also verified by the right means – the uncontradicted means (prabala pramāṇa). Nowadays artificial flowers look real and real flowers look artificial. The rose bouquet in the friend's house looked and smelt real but turned out to be artificial. The roses in the flower market looked too perfect to be real and had no fragrance, but were real. Here touch was the right means to verify the knowledge. Once I got fooled even by the touch when the real leaves were wax-coated and looked artificially real or really artificial! I had to rely on the shopkeeper's words to determine its nature!

Having verified the knowledge, the intellect has to decide what to do.

Many use wrong means to know. 'I disbelieve in the existence of God as it cannot be proved by scientific method.' Scientific methods are not the way to determine the existence of God just as scientific methods are not the way to appreciate the beauty of poetry.

Many use the wrong means to verify the knowledge. The town gossip cannot be relied on to give correct information.

Many take the wrong decision or cannot decide what should be done after they have verified knowledge. A man continues smoking despite the x-ray showing a growth in the lung, in the hope that the x-ray is wrong.

Just as attachment is the weakness of the mind, confusion, indecision, dullness and doubt are the faults of the intellect. Also, when the senses do not perceive well or the mind is attached it gives a wrong picture to the intellect, which is then unable to come to the right decision.

What should the intellect consider the valid means for deciding on worldly matters?

व्यवहारे चिकित्सादिशास्त्राणि विविधानि स्युः।
उपयोगं नरस्तेषां यथा कुर्यात्परिस्थितिः ॥ १२ ॥

vyavahāre cikitsādi-śāstrāṇi vividhāni syuḥ,
upayogaṁ naras-teṣāṁ yathā kuryāt-paristhitiḥ. (12)

व्यवहारे – in the world; चिकित्सा-आदि – medicine and so on; शास्त्राणि – sciences; विविधानि – various; स्युः – exist; उपयोगम् – use; नरः – man; तेषाम् – their; यथा – as; कुर्यात् – should do; परिस्थितिः – situation

12. In the world there are various sciences such as medicine and so on. Man should make use of them as per need or situation.

There is a science or an authority for all secular subjects and transactional matters in the world. They should be considered the right means for deciding on those matters.

A man went to a lawyer with a medical problem. He was advised to go to a doctor and thereafter sent a bill for his advice! A nephrologist cannot answer our dental problems. There are specialists who should be consulted for their specific field of expertise.

Even though this seems obvious, people do ask for advice from ill-informed friends. Many of us in India have been led astray whilst travelling by asking a passer-by for directions. Everyone in India claims to be an expert and advises a varied choice of medicines and cures when we fall sick. Many consider knowledge gathered from google as gospel truth. In modern times anything is sold with the words, 'research has proved ...' No one enquires about the validity of the research, like the pizza company sponsored research, declares that pizzas are healthy.

Therefore to decide on worldly matters the intellect should be guided by the sciences and authority of that field. However sometimes what is needed is simple common sense and native wisdom. The only person without an umbrella on a rainy day was the expert working in the weather department! Another expert asked the village boy how he knew it would rain. The boy said, 'My cow told me so!'

How should the intellect decide upon ethical and spiritual matters?

श्रुतिः स्मृतिश्च धर्मादौ वेदान्तो ब्रह्मदर्शने ।
प्रमाणं विद्यते साक्षात् किमन्येन प्रयोजनम् ॥ १३ ॥

śrutiḥ smṛtiśca dharmādau vedānto brahma-darśane,
pramāṇaṁ vidyate sākṣāt kim-anyena prayojanam. (13)

श्रुतिः – Vedas; स्मृतिः – Smṛtis; च – and; धर्म-आदौ – in Dharma (righteousness) and so on; वेदान्तः – Vedānta; ब्रह्मदर्शने – in realising the absolute Reality (Brahman); प्रमाणम् – means of knowledge; विद्यते – are found; साक्षात् – authoritative; किम् – what; अन्येन – by other (means); प्रयोजनम् –use/need

13. Vedas and Smṛtis are authoritative means to know Dharma (righteousness) and Vedānta (Upaniṣads) for realising the absolute Reality (Brahman). Such being the case, what is the need of any other means of knowledge (pramāṇa)?

The Constitution: How do we understand what is legal or illegal, constitutional or unconstitutional in a country? We cannot learn about this by seeing or inferring. It would be unwise to find that by doing something illegal. Ignorance of the law is no excuse for breaking it. It is our duty as citizens to know the laws or rules and when we break them we are punished. The laws of the land are given in its constitution. It applies to everybody who lives in the country – its citizens and even visitors. I cannot build a house anywhere I find an empty plot and I cannot build a house whatever way I want. I have the freedom of design and material, size and shape as long as it follows local building laws and bye-laws.

Dharma Śāstra: I am not the body, mind and intellect but the indwelling soul (jīva), a part of this universe. In its eternal journey the jīva has assumed this body, mind and intellect which is guided by the constitution of the land. But what is the guide for the soul? How should we decide what is right and wrong, moral or immoral, merit or sin in our life? By what laws should we live so that we do the right thing and avoid sin. These laws are called dharma and the scriptures that speak of them are called Dharma Śāstras. The Śrutis or the Vedas are the supreme means for Dharma.[1]

[1] *dharmaṁ jijñāsamānānāṁ pramāṇaṁ paramaṁ śrutiḥ*

Śrī Kṛṣṇa tells Arjuna that the scriptures (śruti and smṛti) are the valid means of knowledge for dharma (what should be done and not done). One should know them and act accordingly.[1] A man with a bump on the head was asked how he got it. He said, 'You see that door. I didn't!' We should first see (know) and then translate the knowledge into action.

There are many other Dharma Śāstras like Manu Smṛti, Gautama Smṛti, Parāśara Smṛti, Āpastamba Smṛti, Dharma Nirṇaya, Dharma Sindhu and so on. Scriptures of different religions also guide their followers in these matters. The most famous Hindu scripture, the *Bhagavad-gītā* is applicable to all mankind. The basic principles of right living should be learnt from the Dharma Śāstras.

Dharma Gurus: Who will teach me the scriptures? Can I google the information? There are so many scriptures. Do I need to study all of them?

The basic principles of healthy living should be known and followed by all, but when we have a medical problem, we do not sit to study all the books

[1] *tasmāt-śāstraṁ pramāṇaṁ te kāryākāryavyavasthitau,*
jñātvā śāstra-vidhānoktaṁ karma kartum-ihārhasi – *Gītā*-16.24

on medical science. Some people look for medical cures through google, which might get them into more problems. A sensible person will consult a doctor, learn about the problem and follow the prescribed cure.

Similarly Dharma Śāstras and matters of dharma should be learnt from experts in that field, the Dharma Gurus. Not only have they studied the scriptures but they have lived and verified the knowledge. Their minds are pure, detached and subtle and they can objectively and lovingly guide us.

Vedānta Śāstras: Am I only a finite individual (jīva) travelling through lives with different bodies? How can I decide still subtler matters of life like – Who am I? What is my true nature? What is real and unreal? Is there an absolute Truth or is everything only changing? Vedānta is the means that guides us in these subtle spiritual matters.

Studying history books cannot teach me about literature, nor can history verify or authenticate the beauty of literature. They are different fields of knowledge and each has its means of knowing and methods of proving. Since literature cannot be known through scientific experiments it cannot be called unscientific or illogical.

Similarly spiritual knowledge has to be known through spiritual scriptures. Science can neither authenticate nor verify spiritual knowledge. That does not make spiritual knowledge unscientific or illogical. Many wish to prove the existence of God/ Truth through science. Many feel that spiritual knowledge should be taught in a scientific way and that spirituality needs to be authenticated by science to hold its own. It is indeed illogical and unscientific to seek knowledge, authenticity and verification of spiritual matters through science and scientific methods.

Science deals with matter and laws governing matter, however abstract they be. Their instruments are sophisticated and precise, their methods are scientific and logical and their results are praiseworthy. However spirituality talks of the very subject – Self – which observes, thinks and discovers scientific truths. The subject 'I' cannot be known as an object of knowledge. How can I see the eye that sees with the microscope or telescope? Spirituality speaks of the Truth which is beyond the body, senses, mind and intellect. To know this Truth, we will have to study Vedānta. It has its own unique method of revealing the Truth.

Vedānta thus stands on its own feet. It does not need validation from any other field of knowledge. Vedānta is not a mere philosophy, one amongst many other philosophies, but the valid means for Self-knowledge or knowledge of the Truth. Thousands of people through the ages have realised the Truth and validated its authenticity. Study of Vedānta is sufficient in realising the Truth. What is needed is a pure, focussed and subtle mind.

So our intellect should decide on matters of dharma through the Dharma Śāstras and about spiritual matters through Vedānta.

The Body of Intellect

There is a beautiful description in the *Taittirīya Upaniṣad* about the role and right functioning of the intellect. The intellectual sheath (vijñānamaya kośa) is explained metaphorically as a body with various limbs. Faith is its head, ṛtam and satyam are its right and left sides, abidance is its trunk and the total intellect is its support.[1]

Faith is its head: The intellect should be headed and guided by faith. Faith is commonly misunderstood to be a blind, unreasonable emotion, a sentiment unbecoming and unnecessary to a rational intellect. It is not so. Faith is an intellectual ability possessed by all. An atheist has faith in his theory of 'no God' and a rationalist has faith in the rationale of his own intellect. Its position in the knowledge process is primary.

We must have faith that the knowledge exists and most importantly in the validity of the means of knowledge. If we do not have faith that Vedānta is the valid means of knowing the Truth, how can we know the Truth? Did we not have faith in the school teacher and the text books when we studied various subjects in school?

It is therefore said that one with faith, gains knowledge.[2] Learning is the pursuit of truth. Faith

[1] *tasya śraddhaiva śiraḥ, ṛtaṁ dakṣiṇaḥ pakṣaḥ,*
satyam-uttaraḥ pakṣaḥ, yoga ātmā, mahaḥ pucchaṁ pratiṣṭhā
– *Taittirīya Upaniṣad*-2.4

[2] *śraddhāvān-labhate jñānam* – *Gītā*-4.39

has the ability to hold or support the truth (śrat, sat dhatte iti śraddhā). For knowledge to expand we need sāttvika or pure faith, unpolluted by doubts, selfishness and pettiness. We need faith in the existence of God, the validity of Vedānta, the goodness of man, in oneself and noble goals.

In the present time, there is an information boom. There are more graduates, specialists, experts, greater scientific and technological advancement, but lesser faith in oneself, the world and in the Supreme. Knowledge bereft of faith is headless and leads man to trouble. People get PhDs but have no faith in what they write and publish. It is done to get jobs and promotions. The scriptures urge us to have faith (śraddhatsva).

Truth is the right (ṛtam) and left (satyam) sides: Superficially ṛtam and satyam mean the same – the truth. However ṛtam is to ascertain the truth and satyam is to respect and live by it (tad āviṣkaraṇam). Knowledge could be false, deceptive, unreliable or fleeting. We should be able to ascertain its nature (ṛtam) and reject or accept it as per our understanding (satyam). That knowledge which is protected and based on truth alone will lead to true progress.

Abidance (yoga) is the trunk: Various theories and fields of knowledge, variety of goals and pleasures, keep the modern man running helter and skelter. He becomes a jack of all and master of none, distracted in mind and effort.

Deep commitment, regular practise and abidance in the knowledge alone gives it maturity, strength and depth. Dedication and abidance therefore form the main body of knowledge.

The Total intellect – (maha) are its feet or support: We stand on our feet. We move forward in life due to them. An individual's knowledge is limited, but the Total intellect is infinite. Knowledge is strength. The Total intellect being omniscient is also omnipotent. When the individual intellect is in tune with the Totality it expands in vision and knowledge and gains infinite power. Einstein said, 'I want to know the mind of God. All else is mere details.' When we lose sight of the Total, we become narrow-minded, fanatic and petty. A national leader should not think only about his party or his state but about the whole country.

A scientist feels that science has an answer to everything and a politician is convinced that politics can solve world problems. However a holistic vision will help us see the whole picture. Vedānta gives us such a holistic picture of oneself, the world and the Truth.

An intellect endowed with all these limbs becomes a true guide in our life.

The ego is subtler than the intellect. Vedānta says that I am not the ego. But without the ego (I notion), I am nothing. It seems difficult to understand how this knowledge can be lived as we go about our day-to-day interactions with the world. The next verse starts with the explanation of what is the ego.

अहङ्कारः स विज्ञेयस्तादात्म्येन हि जायते ।
देहादिभिर्गुणैः साकं यो विभाति तथा तथा ॥ १४ ॥

ahaṅkāraḥ sa vijñeyas-tādātmyena hi jāyate,
dehādibhir-guṇaiḥ sākaṁ yo vibhāti tathā tathā. (14)

अहङ्कारः – the ego; सः – that; विज्ञेयः – should be known; तादात्म्येन – by identification (with body and so on); हि – alone; जायते – is born; देह-आदिभिः – with the body and so on; गुणैः –with the qualities; साकम् – together with; यः – which; विभाति – appears; तथा तथा – as that and that

14. Know the ego to be that which arises from identification with body and so on and their properties appearing as that and that (thing and quality).

Our entire life is spent in boosting our ego. I seek name, fame, wealth, power and position to become something or someone. We find people looking here and there as they walk with their dogs, seeking attention and recognition through their pets. They write a long list of degrees and positions behind their names, including ex-president of 'y' club and so on.

So is the ego a problem? My ego may be a problem to others, as others' ego is to me, but it does not seem to be problem to me. However, we are told to renounce the ego, destroy the ego or sublimate the ego. It is made out to be something bad and undesired. So what is the ego?

Ego is the notion of individuality that arises when I identify with something. I become one with the thing and its characteristics become me. My individuality keeps changing with whatever I identify with.

When I identify with the body and its characteristics, I say, 'I am a human being, a man, tall and fair, young and handsome ...' When I identify with the mind, I say, 'I am good, happy, sensitive, angry ...' When I identify with the intellect, I say, 'I am intelligent, creative, confused ...' When I identify with the activities of the body-mind-intellect, I say, 'I am seeing, feeling, thinking ...' When I identify with those related to my body, I say, 'I am a brother, father, friend, enemy ...' Identified with any education or profession, I say, 'I am an unemployed and unemployable engineer ...'

The ego arises and thrives with each thing it identifies with, however insignificant it is. Śrī Ramana Maharshi gives the autobiography of the ego saying, 'The ego is born through identification with form, it remains or stays, well-established in forms, it eats or enjoys identifying with forms, it takes on new forms and gives up old forms all the time, whilst itself remaining formless. But it disappears like a ghost when enquired into.'[1]

A typical application form or biodata enlists what the ego identifies with. Name: Ramesh Patel, Age: 30, Gender: Male, Nationality: Indian, Academic Qualification: MBBS, Presently Employed: ABC Hospital, Marital Status: Single ... and so on.

[1] *rūpodbhavo rūpatatipratiṣṭhaḥ rūpāśano dhūtagrihītarūpaḥ,*
svayaṁ virūpaḥ svavicārakāle dhāvaty-ahaṅkāra piśāca eṣaḥ.
– *Saddarśana*-27

Obviously without this identification or individuality we cannot function or exist. Even a Realised Master says I am hungry, tired and sleepy. So is the ego a problem, a boon or a necessary evil?

अहङ्कारस्तु द्विविधो बन्धरूपश्च मुक्तिदः ।
पूज्यभावश्चात्मनीह कर्ता भोक्ता स बन्धकः ॥ १५ ॥

ahaṅkārastu dvividho bandha-rūpaśca muktidaḥ,
pūjya-bhāvaścātmanīha kartā bhoktā sa bandhakaḥ. (15)

अहङ्कारः – ego; तु – also; द्विविधः – (is of) two kinds; बन्धरूपः – (one is) of the nature of bondage; च – and; मुक्तिदः – (the other) releasing; पूज्यभावः – over-estimation; च – and; आत्मनि – in one's own self; इह – here; कर्ता – the notion of doership; भोक्ता – the notion of enjoyership; सः – that (ego); बन्धकः – the cause for bondage

15. The ego is of two kinds, one binding and the other releasing. Overestimation of one's own self and the notion of doership and enjoyership become the cause of bondage.

Everything in the world has two sides – the good and the bad. The ego is also of two types –

The bad news first: It is this ego that binds and causes sorrow. One with such an ego can further be categorised as –

The Egotist: The ego is the notion of individuality which arises when I identify with the body-mind-intellect and its characteristics. This is common in all. However, when this ego is pampered, strengthened and becomes bloated, then a person becomes an egotist, dictatorial, arrogant, self-centered and proud. He feels, 'I am better than everyone, I am always right, I know everything, I deserve to be honoured and worshipped, Do it my way or hit the highway, The world is for my pleasure, I am not answerable to anyone ...' and so on. The egotist is like a one man band. He sings his own praises and blows his own trumpet. He loves to hear people praising and applauding him. The proud mosquito tells its friend, 'Every time I enter a hall, there is loud clapping.'

Everyone has a self-image. The proud man has an exaggerated self-image and an overestimation of himself and his abilities. Some feel superior and others have an inferiority complex. Both are expressions of a strong ego.

The man feels superior to a woman, the rich look down on the poor, the Caucasian thinks he belongs to a superior race, the brahmin feels he is God-sent and the renunciate feels proud of his renunciation.

So where is the problem? What goes up must come down. When the ego is pricked, the person gets hurt, feels insulted and humiliated. Proud people are often lonely and a dictator is hated by many. All time and efforts are wasted in strengthening the ego and maintaining its puffed up image. Others are troubled by our ego and we become the laughing stock when the ego gets punctured. It surely brings sorrow and agitation as it is based on false notions.

The Doership-Enjoyership: Vedānta says that I am not the body-mind-intellect and so I cannot be the doer of actions performed by the body-mind-intellect. However the ego identifies with their activity giving rise to the notion of doership (ahaṁ karomi iti ahaṅkāraḥ). The body moves, eyes see, the mind feels and the intellect thinks, but I say, 'I walk, I see, I feel and I think'.

So what is the problem? The doer (kartā) himself becomes the enjoyer or sufferer (bhoktā) of the results of action. Śrī Ramana Maharshi says that man feels I am the doer and this binds him to become the enjoyer or sufferer of results.[1]

Many ask, "Why am I suffering? What did I do?" If we were shown what we have done, we would realise that the compassionate Lord who presides over all actions and ordains the results, softens the blows we deserve to get.

It is the identification alone that causes problems. When we realise that the 'doer' is a role I play with respect to the action, I would not suffer as much. Suppose an actor forgets that he is playing the role of a beggar and actually feels he is a beggar, it would cause him and others a lot of problem.

A young man at the airport saw that a beautiful woman had left her bag and she went through security check. He picked up the bag and proceeded for security check with the hope of meeting her. He was asked to open the bag by the security guards and to

[1] *karomi karmeti naro vijānan bādhyo bhavet karmaphalaṁ ca bhoktum*
– *Saddarśana*-40

his horror, they found that there were drugs in it. He then had to suffer the subsequent results in the jail for identifying what was not his as his.

The enjoyment or suffering of the result of actions leave impressions in us (vāsanās) which in turn prompt actions, which reap results, which we have to go through. Thus continues the binding cycle of action-result-vāsanā-action-result- vāsanā-action… Śrī Ramana Maharshi says that in this vast ocean of action, impermanent results cause the fall of man and prevent his progress.[1]

[1] *kṛti mahodadhau patana-kāraṇaṁ, phalam-aśāśvataṁ gati-nirodhakam*
– *Upadeśa Sāra*-2

Vedānta says, I am not the doer (akartā) and I strongly feel, I am the doer (kartā) of all actions. How should this vast gap in thinking be bridged? How do I apply this knowledge of Vedānta in my life?

ईश्वरस्यैव दासोऽहं न परेषां कदाचन ।
मतिरित्थं मोचयति कामनाकर्मबन्धनात् ॥ १६ ॥

īśvarasyaiva dāso'haṁ na pareṣāṁ kadācana,
matir-itthaṁ mocayati kāmanā-karma-bandhanāt. (16)

ईश्वरस्य – God's; एव – alone; दासः – servant; अहम् – I; न कदाचन – never; परेषाम् – of other's; मतिः – attitude; इत्थम् – this; मोचयति – releases; कामना-कर्म-बन्धनात् – from the bondage of desires and karmas

16. 'I am a servant of God alone and never of others.' This attitude releases one from the bondage of desires and karmas.

I am Thy servant: It is difficult to realise that I am not the doer of actions. However, there is a way to overcome the bondage due to the notion of doership.

God is the Lord and Master of all and I am His servant. Since He is the Master, it is He who does everything. How can I be the real doer (mukhya kartā)? I am only an instrument in His hands and therefore the secondary doer (gauṇa kartā). Since He is the primary doer, He alone becomes the enjoyer. This attitude frees me from the bondage of the notion of doership and enjoyership.

The Lord is omniscient and omnipotent, I am a part of Him with little knowledge and little strength. In fact what I call my knowledge and strength is actually His. Then how can I take pride in accomplishing anything? How can I feel superior or inferior to anyone, for they too are a part of the Lord like me.

I work with His strength and His knowledge to accomplish His work. The servant works only to please the Master. He has no will or wish of His own. The driver takes the car wherever the Master wishes to go. When actions are done without likes and dislikes, ego and selfishness, they cannot bind the doer.

Śrī Hanumānajī exemplifies this attitude of being a servant (dāsa bhāva). When asked how he accomplished such difficult tasks like crossing the ocean, finding Sītājī, facing Rāvaṇa and torching Laṅkā, he smiled and said, 'It is the Lord who did all. I was only His messenger and servant.' Bharata considered the kingdom as Śrī Rāma's and ruled Ayodhya as Śrī Rāma's representative till His arrival. However Rāvaṇa tried to compete with Lord Śrī Rāma and got killed.

So the best way to overcome the bondage of the ego is to become the vehicle or instrument (karaṇa) of the Lord and allow the Lord to function through us. The flute in the hands of Lord Śrī Kṛṣṇa makes itself hollow, free of all ego and pride, and allows the Flute-bearer to play His divine music through it. No wonder it became the envy of all and the favourite of the Lord.

Vedānta says that I am not the body, mind, intellect and the ego. Then who am I?

देहादिभ्यः उपाधिभ्यः परात्मा भिन्न एव सः ।
सच्चिदानन्दरूपोऽयं ब्रह्मरूपः सनातनः ॥ १७ ॥

dehādibhyaḥ upādhibhyaḥ parātmā bhinna eva saḥ,
saccidānanda-rūpo'yaṁ brahma-rūpaḥ sanātanaḥ. (17)

देह-आदिभ्यः – from body and so on; उपाधिभ्यः – from all conditionings; परात्मा – the Supreme Self; भिन्नः – different; एव – indeed; सः – that (Self); सच्चिदानन्दरूपः – of the nature of Existence-Consciousness-Bliss; अयम् – this (Ātman); ब्रह्मरूपः – the infinite Truth (Brahman); सनातनः – eternal

17. The Self (Ātman) is verily distinct from all conditionings of body and so on. It is Existence-Consciousness-Bliss, eternal and one with the infinite Truth (Brahman).

Known to the Unknown: The method of Vedānta is to lead us from the known to the unknown. We are guided to think based on the śruti – the statement of the Upaniṣads, yukti – logic and reasoning and anubhūti – experience of the wise and our own experience. I feel I am the body-mind-intellect. That is known and experienced, but the knower is different from the known. The body-mind-intellect are known to me. I am therefore different from the body-mind-intellect. Then who am I other than the body, mind and intellect?

There seems to be two I's – the 'individual I' born from identification with the body-mind-intellect and the 'knower I' which illumines them. Since I am the knower and not the known, I am not the individual I (jīvātmā), but different (para) I (ātmā).

Also the body-mind-intellect is finite or limited in time and space. The ego born through identification with the finite is also finite. If I am not the finite self (jīvātmā), but different from it, then I must be infinite (para-ātmā), unlimited by time and space.

Conditioned and Unconditioned: The body, mind and intellect are called conditioning adjuncts (upādhi). It is defined as that which remains near something and superimposes its characteristics on the thing, without bringing about any intrinsic change in the thing (upa samīpe sthitvā svīyaṁ rūpam anyatra ādadhāti iti upādhi).

A crystal is kept near a blue cloth. It appears blue without actually becoming blue. Later if a red cloth is kept, it appears red again without actually becoming red. Even when it looked blue or red, it was neither. It always remains colourless and crystal clear. The blue and red cloth are called its conditionings (upādhi).

University degrees are also called upādhis in some Indian languages. They seem to add titles and arrogance without bringing any change or knowledge in the student! Mark Twain is supposed to have said, 'I did not let education interfere with my learning!'

Diseases in the body are called ādhi. Mental agitations and problems are called vyādhi and intellectual conditionings are called upādhis. The way out of their identification is samādhi or meditation on the Self, which is different from them. Thus by enquiry and meditation we can reach a state of absorption in the Self (samādhi). That Self in which the mind is absorbed is also called samādhi.

The body-mind-intellect and their characteristics cannot bring about any changes in the Self. It remains ever the same pure and unconditioned. The body may be healthy or diseased, the mind may be saintly or criminal, the intellect may be bright or dull, but the Self is never affected by them.

What is the nature of the unconditioned Self?

Existence-Consciousness-Bliss: Conditioned by the body or mind, I say, 'I am tall', I am happy'. Free from these conditioning, I just 'am'– pure unconditioned existence. 'I am' is present in all experiences. I can never experience my own absence or non-existence. I exist and therefore everything else exists. I am the eternal, infinite Existence.

I am and I am conscious that I am. The knower is Consciousness and the known inert. I am the eternal infinite knower Consciousness, which illumines all experiences and the body-mind-intellect. Since the infinite Self is one alone, I am the eternal Existence-Consciousness.

That which is finite or limited gives sorrow. That which is infinite gives bliss.[1] The infinite Self is therefore Bliss absolute unconditioned by the body-mind-intellect.

I am therefore the eternal Existence-Consciousness-Bliss which is called Brahman, the Truth or Reality. Due to ignorance a person thinks he is the body. When he enquires, he says, 'I am the body with a soul.' Further enquiry makes him understand that inside the body is the mind, within which is the intellect and within it a soul, within which exists God/Self/Truth. It is not that the body has a Self, but actually I am the infinite Self/Truth having a body-mind-intellect.

[1] *yo vai bhūmā tat-sukhaṁ na-alpe sukham-asti.*
– *Chāndogya Upaniṣad*-7.23.1

How can I translate the knowledge that I am Existence-Consciousness-Bliss Absolute into my daily life?

ज्ञानेनैतेन शास्त्रस्य जगत्यस्मिंश्च सर्वदा ।
आनन्दस्वामिनः सन्तु लोका नानन्दयाचकाः ॥ १८ ॥

jñānenaitena śāstrasya jagatyasmiṁśca sarvadā,
ānanda-svāminaḥ santu lokā nānanda-yācakāḥ. (18)

ज्ञानेन – with knowledge; एतेन – with this; शास्त्रस्य – of scriptures; जगति – in the world; अस्मिन् – in this; च – and; सर्वदा – always; आनन्दस्वामिनः – masters of happiness; सन्तु – may (they) be; लोकाः – people; न – not; आनन्दयाचकाः – beggars of happiness

18. Endowed with this scriptural knowledge, may all men ever be the masters of happiness and not the beggars of happiness.

My relative identity is the individual identified with the body-mind-intellect (jīvātmā), but my absolute and true identity is Existence-Consciousness-Bliss. How do I live it? I do not have to proclaim it to the world or change my name in the passport as Brahman. A child's T-shirt had BATMAN written on it. A crease in the shirt made me read it as B ATMAN (Be the Pure Self), which I felt was sound advise for all.

I am of the nature of eternal Existence (sat-svarūpa), so I should live and let live. I should not kill or harm other beings. Being of the nature of Consciousness and Knowledge Principle (cit-svarūpa), I should live consciously with knowledge and dispel ignorance in others. I should not cheat others. Since I am Bliss Absolute (ānanda-svarūpa), I should be happy and make others happy. Existence is Consciousness and Existence-Consciousness is Bliss. I am one alone without a second (advaita-svarūpa), so I should live in unity and harmony and not create any differences.

The Master: I am Bliss Absolute, the very source of happiness. Therefore my happiness does not depend on worldly objects, beings or circumstances, or the condition of my body or mind. I am the master and not the beggar of joy. I should therefore not ask or crave for things with the expectation of happiness. Whether in meditation or in the midst of pleasure, in the company of people or all alone, the Realised

Master is ever in Bliss.[1] Change in the set-up of things should not upset me.

Whenever I find myself fearful, unhappy or tense, I must realise that it is because of identification with the not-self and attachments. Interestingly we are attached to inert things like money, but money is not attached to anyone. It changes hands easily and leaves us to go even into our enemy's pocket. Man is enslaved by wealth, but wealth is a slave to none.[2]

Some people are anānanda (never happy), others are kadānanda (waiting to become happy and wondering when they will become happy), yet others yadākadānanda (sometimes happy, sometimes sad), but we should be sadānanda (always happy) as Happiness is my true nature. A renunciate is called svāmī – a Master or mahārāja – a great king, as he is happy despite circumstances. Also, the names of svāmīs end with ānanda. A child translated my name, Swami Tejomayananda, as Master Brilliant Joy.

1 *yogarato vā bhogarato vā saṅgarato vā saṅgavihīnaḥ,*
yasya brahmaṇi ramate cittaṁ nandati nandati nandatyeva
– *Bhaja Govindam*-19

2 *arthasya puruṣo dāsaḥ, artho dāso na kasyacit*

A king was told that he would be happy if he wore the shirt of a happy man. A search party was sent throughout the kingdom but everyone had some unhappiness or the other. Finally they found a person who seemed truly happy, but he was shirtless! He was brought to the court and asked what made him happy. He said, 'Happy with a shirt, happy without a shirt!'

With the understanding that I am the source of happiness, I should live like a Master and not like a beggar in this world.

Now we come to the important and universally debated topic of God. Does God exist? If so, who is He, where is He and how is He related to me?

ईश्वरः सर्वभूतानां सर्वदा हृदि वर्तते ।
तदन्तर्यामिरूपेण सर्वभूतसुहृत्तया ॥ १९ ॥

īśvaraḥ sarvabhūtānāṁ sarvadā hṛdi vartate,
tad-antaryāmi-rūpeṇa sarvabhūta-suhṛttayā. (19)

ईश्वरः – God; सर्वभूतानाम् – of all beings; सर्वदा – ever; हृदि – in the hearts; वर्तते – exists; तत् – that; अन्तर्यामिरूपेण – as the inner controller; सर्वभूत-सुहृत्तया – as the well-wisher of all beings

19. God ever exists in the hearts of all beings as their inner controller and well-wisher.

Talk of God: God is the most talked about and written about entity from time immemorial. The maximum search, even on google, is for God. Since He is not experienced like any other worldly object, even His existence becomes a matter of faith. There is a debate about every aspect of Him, including His very existence. There are extremes of fanatic believers to staunch non-believers with many shades of believers and disbelievers in between.

Simple Faith in God: Some with simple faith have no doubt about the existence of God. They may not have studied the scriptures, but they do not need their belief to be authenticated by the scriptures. They do not need logic or proof of His existence. They know deep within that He exists, that He is kind, compassionate and that He listens to their prayers. Such people directly experience His presence and blessings and therefore their belief is firm and abiding. However the faith of those who do not feel His presence or blessings strongly can get shaken by personal tragedies or strong arguments of disbelievers.

Faith in Scriptures: The scriptures give knowledge about God – who He is, what He does and so on. Those with abiding faith in the scriptures also have faith in God. Their faith is backed by knowledge and authority of scriptures and is therefore not easily shaken even when they do not feel His presence strongly, have personal tragedies or by arguments of disbelievers.

Faith in Guru: Sages and saints, Gurus and Realised Masters also speak about God and His role in life. They speak from the scriptures and their own direct experience. Those with strong faith in them, also have faith in God. Their faith is stronger as it has the authority of the scriptures and the Guru's experience becomes the proof of God. They see the effect of faith in the Guru. They too remain unshaken in tragedies or by arguments of the disbelievers.

Faith in Oneself: Our perception, observation and analysis gives us knowledge of this world. Those who are rationalists, who have faith in their intellect too can infer and understand the existence and nature of God. They may not have faith in the words of the scriptures or Gurus but their own reasoning makes them believers in God. Their well thought out logic remains unshaken when challenged by non-believers.

Little Faith: Some are not sure of their faith in God. They do not have the guts to be non-believers nor do they have faith enough to be true believers.

A man who went to heaven told a communist on his return that he saw God in heaven. The communist said, 'I thought as much.' He later met a priest and told him that there was no God in heaven. The priest said, 'I thought as much!'

Partial Faith: Some have faith in some parts of the scriptures, maybe the Karma Kāṇḍa of the Vedas, so they perform rituals with faith. They may not believe or have interest in the Jñāna Kāṇḍa or the knowledge section. Some have faith in certain aspects of God, like His existence and omnipotence, but not in His justice and compassion. Such partial faith has but partial benefit.

Faithless: Some do not believe in God as it is fashionable to be non-believers or it is considered intellectual. Some have just not thought about God. Some others are truly atheists through their own logic and thinking. Rabindranath Tagore is believed to have said, 'I like God because He gives me the freedom to deny His existence.' Interestingly logic is a double edged sword which can be used to disprove and prove the existence of God.

The Rationale of God's Existence and nature: Logic strengthens our faith. Here we shall give easy to follow logic without going into pedantic or scholarly discussions.

God, the Creator (sarva-kartā): We see in the world that something does not come out of nothing. Every effect must have a cause. Creation too must have a creator. This endless expanse of world must have an infinite Creator. This infinite Creator of the world is called God in religion and Truth in philosophy.

God, the uncreated: A finite thing (gross or subtle) or a part (however big) of the world cannot be the ultimate cause of the world. Also, the cause preceeds the effect. The infinite God/Truth alone can be the ultimate cause, the cause of all causes of creation. Since He existed before creation, He is the uncreated cause of all. The question, 'who created God', is thus unanswered.

Some people think of God as a concept and therefore claim that He was created by the human intellect. Concepts of God are creations of human intellect, but God/Truth is not a concept but the ultimate cause of all concepts.

God, the material and sentient cause (abhinna-nimitta-upādāna-kāraṇa): A clay pot is made of clay by the potter. Both the clay and the potter are needed to create the pot and must exist before the pot was created. Everything created must have a material (clay) and a sentient (potter) cause. God/Truth existed before creation, so God/Truth must be both the material and the sentient cause of the world.

God, the all-pervading (sarva-vyāpī): The clay becomes and pervades the pot made from it. The material cause becomes and pervades the effect. God creates the world out of Himself and becomes the world. Being all He pervades all.

God, the omniscient and omnipotent (sarvajña and sarva-śaktimān): The potter has the knowledge, skill and the strength needed to make the pot. The creator of a finite object has finite knowledge and strength. God/Truth, the Creator of this infinite world must have infinite knowledge (omniscient) and have infinite strength (omnipotent). Also being all, He knows all and all strength seen anywhere is His alone. The strength of every wave is that of the ocean, whose strength is more than all the waves put together.

God is Existence-Consciousness (saccid-svarūpa): The pot exists. It 'is'. Even its absence is experienced as the pot 'is' not. Every thought, feeling and object – gross or subtle – exists, has existence. God/Truth is the Existence Principle because of which everything in the world exists.

Also the presence and the absence of everything is known. God/Truth is the very Knowledge Principle or Consciousness because of which all thoughts, feelings and objects are known.

God, the Intelligent Being: Great intelligence and managerial skills are needed in running a successful multi national company. God is the creator and upholder of all the laws that govern this multi-cosmos universe with innumerable products and beings working day and night. His intelligence, planning and managerial skills are unconceivable.

God, the Ruler of all (sarveśvara): Being all, He rules all. Being the sole monarch, there is none to revolt against Him or His rule. How can the waves oppose or threaten the rule of the ocean? They cannot banish the ocean or get banished by the ocean. They can only submit to the rule of the ocean.

God's rule is neither tyrannical nor partial. He is both just and kind so we should lovingly submit to His rule.

God, the Self of all (sarvātmā): The oceanic water alone is the self of the wave, the essence of the wave. What it could call 'I' is but the oceanic water. Similarly God being all, is the very Self of all. He is very close to us, in fact He is our own Self. I love myself the most, so naturally I should love God. The Self in me is the Self in all and so I should love all and serve all.

God presides over all actions (karmādhyakṣa): Actions and the instruments through which they are performed are inert, finite and dependent. Even a fully automated factory must have a programmer (sentient being) who set it up. God is the sentient factor without which no action is possible. All actions – good, bad or ugly – happen in His presence. A Guru asked a disciple to kill a chicken where there was no one. The disciple came back without doing the task saying, 'Wherever I went, I was there and so was the chicken.' God is the Self of all. All actions happen in His presence alone.

God, the giver of results (karmaphaladātā): If we were independent in getting results, we would always get desired results. I would never flunk a test however badly I wrote it. Then I would award myself for my achievements. I would then even decide my own pay scale and promote myself. Do I put myself in the jail when I steal? The teacher gives me the result of my test, based on what I have written. God is the giver of results of our actions based on what we do and with what attitude we do.

God, the inner controller of all (sarvāntaryāmī): The ocean controls the movement of all waves both from within and without. God, being both inside and outside, is the controller of all. He controls us from outside through the laws of nature, laws of the land, social norms and circumstances. He controls us from within through the laws that govern the body-mind-intellect. The food eaten goes into the stomach through peristalsis. We are informed when the stomach is full and if we eat thereafter, the extra food is vomited by reverse peristalsis.

God is independent (svatantra): He is the controller of all, but none can control Him. He wields His creative power (māyā) which acts as per His will (māyāpati). The three qualities of māyā – nobility, activity and inertia (sattva, rajas and tamas) bind all in the world. God is not bound by them and is predominantly endowed with sattva (viśuddha-sattva-guṇa-pradhāna).

A noble person, who is dependent and without much power, cannot help others. Vibhīṣaṇa however noble, could not do much as long as he lived at the mercy of the wicked Rāvaṇa. God is all-powerful, independent and noble.

God, the well-wisher of all (sarva-bhūtahita): Being all, He loves us as His own Self and therefore He is the friend and well-wisher of all. He guides us from within as our conscience. The voice within always tells us what is right and wrong. Even when we do wrong, He does not leave us. Jaya and Vijaya the gate keepers of Vaikuṇṭha, His abode, became arrogant and insulted the saintly Sanat Kumāras. They were punished to become demons on earth, yet the Lord incarnated on earth each time, to save them and others from them. In our good times He walks with us and in our bad times He carries us. He is not just our wish fulfiller, but more importantly our well-wisher.

After knowing about the existence and the nature of God, what should I do?

समोऽयं सर्वभूतेषु निष्पक्षो जलमेघवत्।
तमेव शरणं गत्वा शान्तिमाप्नोति मानवः॥ २०॥

samo'yaṁ sarvabhūteṣu niṣpakṣo jala-meghavat,
tameva śaraṇaṁ gatvā śāntim-āpnoti mānavaḥ. (20)

समः – is same; अयम् – He (God); सर्वभूतेषु – in all beings; निष्पक्षः – impartial; जलमेघवत् – like the water-bearing clouds; तम् – Him; एव – alone; शरणम् – refuge; गत्वा – having sought; शान्तिम् – peace; आप्नोति – attains; मानवः – man

20. He is same in all beings and impartial like the water-bearing clouds (rains). Seeking His refuge alone, man attains peace.

Is God just and impartial? This is a question likely to come to the minds of many. In this world we see that the undeserving take the cake and eat it too and the deserving get crumbs. Some with plenty get even more and those with next to nothing are robbed of what little they have. The learned are neglected and the moneyed are pampered. The petty criminals are jailed and the big ones move about scot free. There seems little justice in this world.

Also, we see that the teachers have their favourites and children always feel that their siblings are loved more by the parents. Like worldly people, does God love those who love Him more? Why does He always side with the good?

God, the same for all (samo'haṁ sarvabhūteṣu): Being all, God is the same in all. But is He the same 'to' all? Lord Śrī Kṛṣṇa says, 'I am the same to all. None are liked or disliked by me.'[1]

God is just: Actions give results in their own time as guided by His laws. The results of past good actions are likely to come to the evil and the results of past bad actions are likely to come to the good. This makes us feel that God is unjust. But His laws are impeccable and God is always just.

God is impartial: The clouds shower rains without partiality. The farmer who has prepared his fields

1 *samo'haṁ sarvabhūteṣu na me dveṣyo'sti na priyaḥ – Gītā-9.29*

and sown the seeds reaps a good crop. Another who has neglected his field reaps grass and weeds. God is similarly impartial. Also it rains equally on the houses of all. One harvests the water and one allows it to drain away. Similarly God blesses all equally.

Even though He is the same to all, all are not the same to Him and that makes a difference. The fire gives warmth to all. Those who stay away from it, shiver with cold and those who come near, get its warmth.

Both Arjuna and Duryodhana went to Lord Śrī Kṛṣṇa to seek His help in the war. He asked them to choose between Himself and His army. Arjuna chose the Lord and Duryodhana chose His army, and lost the war.

During Tretā Yuga, Sugrīva the son of Sun-god befriended Lord Śrī Rāma and was protected against Vālī, the son of Indra. Whereas during the *Mahābhārata* war in Dvāpara Yuga, the Lord as Śrī Kṛṣṇa sided with Arjuna, the son of Indra, against Karṇa the son of the Sun-god. The Lord is indeed impartial towards all beings, be they human beings or deities.

Knowing the nature of God, we should take refuge in Him and seek Him alone. Śaraṇa means both refuge and goal.

God, the refuge: When it rains we run for shelter. The shelter protects us from the onslaught of rain. Similarly God protects those who take refuge in Him when they are in trouble.

The cow-heard boys of Gokula and Vrindavan called Śrī Kṛṣṇa whenever they were in trouble or even if they were hungry. God made arrangement for their food. When there was heavy rain due to the wrath of Indra, they again asked Śrī Kṛṣṇa to save them. The Lord lifted the Govardhana mountain and sheltered the entire village.

I know of a lady whose daughter had a terrible accident in another country. Knowing that she could do little from far away at that time, she prayed to God. 'You are all-pervading. So You are also where she is. I cannot go there immediately. So You be with her and take care of her.'

God the goal: All seek happiness. God is Bliss Absolute and so He is the goal of all. We should therefore seek Him alone and consider Him alone as our ultimate goal of life.

The meaning of śaraṇāgati is further explained in the next verse.

ईश्वरेच्छातिरिक्ता मे मा भूयात्कामना कदा ।
एषा मतिर्हि भक्तस्य शरणागतिरिष्यते ॥ २१ ॥

īśvarecchātiriktā me mā bhūyāt-kāmanā kadā,
eṣā matir-hi bhaktasya śaraṇāgatir-iṣyate. (21)

ईश्वर-इच्छा – the will of God; **अतिरिक्ता** – other than; **मे** – to me; **मा** – not; **भूयात्** – happen; **कामना** – desire; **कदा** – any time; **एषा** – this; **मतिः** – thought; **हि** – surely; **भक्तस्य** – of a devotee; **शरणागतिः** – surrender; **इष्यते** – is called

21. 'May I have no desire other than the will of God.' This thought of a devotee is called surrender.

'Thine will be done, not mine, not mine': This is the meaning of surrender. Initially we may have our own personal desires and seek specific results also. But when our desires are not fulfilled or when we do not get as we specify, we should accept what we get as the will of God. We generally accept undesired results with complaints, cursings, resignation or as 'sour grapes'. When we see the hand of God, behind all we get, our attitude is of cheerful and reverential acceptance. Saint Mīrābāī saw the hand of God behind the poison sent by her husband and danced as she drank it.[1] The poison turned to nectar.

As the mind becomes pure, all desires also are surrendered to God. Saint Tulasīdāsa said, 'I am Yours. You shower Your grace in whichever way You want.'[2] Young Prahlāda was asked by the Lord to ask for a boon. He said, 'I have no desires. My life is fulfilled by Your vision.' On insisting, he asked the Lord, 'May there never be desires in me.'

We believe God to be omnipotent and so we pray to Him to fulfil our desires. However we do not accept that He is omniscient. We therefore keep telling Him, 'I want this, that and the other.' We also tell Him what to do and what is good for us!

We should realise that He knows, and He also knows what is best for us, He is kind and compassionate and gives what is best for us. He

1 *viṣa kā pyālā rāṇājī ne bhejā pibata mīrā nācī re*

2 *jo cāhe so kara kṛpā, tero tulasī hai*

is there with us through thick and thin. When we understand this we will surrender to His will.

The husband tells his wife, 'I am yours'. Thereafter she spends his money at will. Similarly when the 'I' is surrendered, my desires and insistences and actions are also surrendered to Him. Thereafter His will alone prevails in our life. Such surrender is not easy and comes with true knowledge, faith and devotion.

After dealing with the topic of the experiencer of the world (jīva) and the Creator of the world (Īśvara), we are introduced to what Vedānta says regarding the experienced world (jagat).

ब्रह्मणः सर्वभूतानि प्रतिभान्ति स्थितानि च ।
तस्मिन्नेव लयं यान्ति सर्ववेदान्तनिश्चयः ॥ २२ ॥

brahmaṇaḥ sarvabhūtāni pratibhānti sthitāni ca,
tasminneva layaṁ yānti sarvavedānta-niścayaḥ. (22)

ब्रह्मणः – from Brahman; **सर्वभूतानि** – all beings; **प्रतिभान्ति** – appear (are born); **स्थितानि** – exist; **च** – and; **तस्मिन्** – in that (Brahman); **एव** – alone; **लयम्** – dissolution; **यान्ति** – attain; **सर्ववेदान्तनिश्चयः** – (this is) the conclusion of all Upaniṣads

22. The firm conclusion of all Upaniṣads is that all beings are born (appear) from Brahman, exist and dissolve in it alone.

People have various opinions of the world. The students were asked in a geography class, 'How is the world?' One of them replied, 'Crooked!' We are generally busy working or enjoying in this world. We get philosophical either when tragedy strikes or when we are in love. Only the thinkers, philosophers, theologists, scientists, religious or spiritual persons think seriously about the world. They ask questions like, 'What is the origin of the world?' Is it real? And so on.

Vedānta says that the world emerges (appears) from, remains in and merges into the Truth (Brahman).

The Origin of the World: We have already seen in the discussion about God that before creation there existed the Truth alone, One without a second.[1] The world originated from this Truth which is infinite Existence-Consciousness-Bliss. The world is made up of time, space and objects (things and beings) with many names, forms and qualities. Since one part of the world cannot be the cause of the world, the Truth must be timeless, spaceless and objectless (nameless, formless, attributeless). This Truth alone is both the material and the sentient cause of the world.

[1] *sadeva somya-idam-agra āsīt-ekam-eva-advitīyam*
– *Chāndogya Upaniṣad*-6.2.1

Some consider the Truth/God to be only the sentient (efficient) cause and not the material cause. Then who created the material and from what? The Truth by definition is infinite and there cannot be two infinites. All is included in the infinite Truth. Therefore the Truth alone can be the material and the sentient cause of the world, the origin of the world or the ultimate cause of the world.

The Sustenance of the World: The waves emerge in the ocean and are sustained by the ocean. Similarly time, space and objects with names, forms and attributes cannot exist without the Truth which is the very Existence Principle from which they emerge. The Truth is the nourisher and the very life and essence of all things and beings of the world. For every change, there must be a changeless substratum. The Truth is the very substratum of this ever-changing world.

The Dissolution of the World: What is born must die. What emerges, must merge back into its origin. The body made up of the five elements, disintegrates into the five elements when we die. We come from dust and die to become dust again. The entire world emerges from the Truth and merges back into the Truth at the time of dissolution.

Innumerable waves are born and merge with the ocean every moment. Similarly, not only at the time of the great dissolution, but every being, every object and every thought emerges and merges into the Truth all the time.

The Nature of the World: How is the world created from the Truth? Milk curdles to become curd (yogurt). The milk changes its nature and becomes curd. Once it has become curd, it is not available as milk anymore. Does the Truth modify to become the world?

The snake vision appears to be seen on the rope. The rope does not actually become the snake or the snake vision. Also names and forms like waves, ripples or tsunami are superimposed on the oceanic water. The water remains H_2O and does not change its watery nature despite the appearance of innumerable waves. Does the Truth appear to become this world? Is the world an appearance?

The world is by nature ever changing and the Truth is by nature, never changing. How can the changeless Truth, change to become the changing world? So the world is not a modification of the Truth, but an appearance on the Truth. Like the changing scenes of the movie on the changeless, spotless, colourless screen, the world appears, appears to remain and the appearance disappears into the pure infinite Truth. Brahman means that which is infinite and that which supports (bṛhattamatvāt, bharaṇāt). The Truth is the infinite substratum of the world. The world is a superimposed appearance on the Truth.

The Dream World: This knowledge is very difficult to understand. Vedānta gives us an example based on our daily experience to explain this fact.

We have all experienced a dream. Who is the creator of the dream – the dreamer and his entire dream world? What is the material with which the dream world is made? What sustains the dream world and where does it disappear? The waking mind alone is the creator, sustainer and destroyer of the entire dream. It alone is the material and sentient cause of the dream. It alone appears as the entire dream – be it a sweet dream or a nightmare.

A woman in her dream, came face to face with a lion. Frightened, she asked the lion, "Will you eat me?" The lion said, "You decide. After all it's your dream!" She alone had become the dream woman and the dream lion.

A man in his dream failed in his exam. When he told his friend about the dream, the friend said, 'You cannot even pass in your dream? After all, you were the one who set the exam paper!'

Being a part of this whole, am I also an appearance? What is my Truth?

आत्मरूपेण तद्ब्रह्म सर्वभूतहृदि स्थितम्।
गूढ भावोऽस्य शास्त्रस्य ज्ञातव्यश्च मुमुक्षुभिः ॥२३॥

ātma-rūpeṇa tadbrahma sarvabhūta-hṛdi sthitam,
gūḍha bhāvo'sya śāstrasya jñātavyaśca mumukṣubhiḥ. (23)

आत्मरूपेण – as their own self; तत् – that; ब्रह्म – Brahman; सर्वभूतहृदि – in the hearts of all beings; स्थितम् – exists; गूढ – deep; भावः – import; अस्य – of this; शास्त्रस्य – of the scriptures; ज्ञातव्यः – must necessarily be understood; च – and; मुमुक्षुभिः – by the seekers of Liberation

23. That Brahman exists in the heart of all beings as their own Self. Seekers of Liberation should understand the deep import of this scriptural statement.

Many are interested in knowing the meaning of their dreams. 'Does the crow sitting on my roof top in my dream mean that I will become rich?' Vedānta teaches us, who is the dreamer, what is a dream, how do we dream and how real is the dream.

The Dream Self: Let us think of the example of the dream a little more. Is the dreamer, dreaming the waker and the waking world? Am I dreaming that I am reading this book? Or, is the waker dreaming the dreamer and the dream world? Either way the dreamer or the waker are a part of the dream and waking world respectively. In case we assume the former, then the waker and the waking world is in the dreamer's mind. If we assume the latter, then the dream and the dream world is in the waker's mind. The latter seems more real to us.

The waker's mind appears as the dream world. Naturally the body-mind-intellect of the dreamer, being part of the dream world are also an appearance. However the essence or the self of the dreamer and all beings in the dream world is the waking mind alone. I dream that I am a clown in a circus. The self or essence of the clown and all the animals and the spectators is the waking mind alone. So essentially I applaud myself for the brilliant performance!

Similarly, the world is an appearance and so are all the names and forms of all the beings in the world. However the essence and the Self of all the beings – be they plant, animal or human – is the Truth alone. All this needs serious thinking as its implication is far reaching.

The import of the previous verse is explained hereafter.

इदं जगद्वस्तुतश्च ब्रह्मभिन्नं न सिध्यति ।
तथैव चात्मभिन्नं वा ब्रह्मात्मैक्यप्रबोधनात् ॥ २४ ॥

idaṁ jagadvastutaśca brahma-bhinnaṁ na sidhyati,
tathaiva cātma-bhinnaṁ vā brahmātmaikya-
prabodhanāt. (24)

इदम् – this; जगत् – world; वस्तुतः – in reality; च – and; ब्रह्मभिन्नम् – as different from Brahman (independent of Brahman); न – cannot; सिध्यति – be known; तथा एव – in the same way; च – also; आत्मभिन्नम् – different from Self (Ātman); वा – nor; ब्रह्म-आत्म-ऐक्य-प्रबोधनात् – because of the establishment of the identity of Brahman and Ātman (in the scriptures)

24. In reality, this world cannot exist different from Brahman and so also from Ātman because the identity of Brahman and Ātman has been established.

Different World: The world of differences is an appearance on the one Truth. So it appears that there are two entities – one, the Truth and other, the world. But are they really different.

One with the world: The rope appears as the snake. One may say there is a rope and a snake, but the snake is not different from the rope. Is the dream different from the waking mind? Even if they are counted as two entities, they are essentially one. The superimposition does not have a separate existence from the substratum. They are essentially one. The Truth appears as the world, but the world is not different from the Truth. The world has no existence other than the Truth. The world is in essence the Truth alone.

One with the Self: The last verse explained that the Truth is not different from the Self. The Self of all beings is indeed the Truth. The knowledge 'I am the infinite Truth' is called the brahmātmaikya-bodha, which is the very essence of Vedānta.

Since the world is in essence the Truth, and I am the Truth, the world is not different from me. Here the 'I' refers not to the finite individual but the pure Self, different from the body-mind-intellect.

This knowledge is staggering and deep in its import. Realising this Truth, man attains Liberation.

What is the result of this knowledge and how should I apply it in my life?

अहं ब्रह्मेति विज्ञानात्कथं मे जगतो भयम् ।
द्वितीयाद्धि भयं भूयात्सर्ववेदान्तघोषितम् ॥ २५ ॥

ahaṁ brahmeti vijñānāt-kathaṁ me jagato bhayam,
dvitīyāddhi bhayaṁ bhūyāt-sarvavedānta-ghoṣitam. (25)

अहम् – I; ब्रह्म – (am) Brahman; इति – as so; विज्ञानात् – by (such) realisation; कथम् – how; मे – to me; जगतः – from the world; भयम् – fear (can come); द्वितीयात् – from duality; हि – alone; भयम् – fear; भूयात् – can arise; सर्ववेदान्तघोषितम् – (this is) the proclamation of all Upaniṣads

25. With the Realisation, 'I am Brahman', how can I have any fear from this world? 'Fear arises from duality alone', is the proclamation of all Upaniṣads.

A different experience: Without the knowledge of Vedānta, how do I see the world? I, the experiencer, experience the world of objects and beings as different from me. How do I interact and respond to the world? The objects and beings in the world invoke feelings of likes, dislikes, love, hate, jealousy, greed, passion, compassion and so on. Some things I consider mine and others, not mine. Some things I desire, some I long for, and some I pant for. A candidate standing for election was asked what were the issues involved in election. He said, 'There are no issues. He has the chair and I want it. It is as simple as that.'

When I see the world as different from me, there is alienation, loneliness and fear. It is interesting that we are scared when there is only one man in the train compartment and are also scared when we are alone in a train compartment. The thought of the other causes fear (dvitīyāt bhayaṁ bhavati).

A unifying experience: Vedānta says that the world is not different from me. It is myself appearing as various things and beings. With this vision how will I see the world? What shall I like or dislike? Whom shall I love or hate? What is mine and yours? What will I run after or away from? Whom will I fear? Sadāśiva Brahmendra said, 'The whole world is the Truth/Self alone. Now what shall I enjoy or not enjoy...?'[1] Profit

[1] *sarvaṁ brahmamayaṁ, kiṁ bhoktavyaṁ, kim abhoktavyam ...*

or loss, victory or failure, honour and dishonour, would mean nothing. So the Realised Master is never argumentative.[1] A scholar wanted to defeat the great saint Kabīradāsa in a debate. The saint told him, 'I accept defeat, why waste our time!'

It is said that before you argue with a foolish person, see that he is not doing the same thing. A logician enjoyed arguing and always won in debate. Once his friend saw him looking sad and asked for the reason. He said, "I was defeated in a debate in my dream." The friend consoled him, "The one who defeated you was also you." The Sufi poet Rumi says, 'If the pictures knew they all came from the same brush, they would get along fine with each other.'

Revisiting the dream experience: Imagine that we are re-entering our dream with the knowledge of the waking mind. The dream world would appear so different. The nightmare and the winning of the lottery in the dream would be equally entertaining. There would be no fear of the ferocious tiger, or pride in winning an award. We would enjoy everything and love everyone as our own Self.

[1] *vijānan ātmā na bhavet ativādī*

Absence of experience: Seeing the world is not a problem, but seeing it as different from me, is the problem. The likes, dislikes, fear and so on are caused not by the experience of the world but due to the notion that the world is different from me. Therefore Vedānta does not insist on the non-perception of the world or attainment of nirvikalpa samādhi, but on the Realisation of the Truth – 'I am the infinite Truth and world is not different from me.'

A king went into the hall of mirrors in his palace. He was entertained by the various images of himself in the concave and convex mirrors of various sizes. However his pet dog, when he entered the hall, was frightened at the hundreds of other dogs barking back at him. Even when the dog was taken out of the room, his fear did not go. He would become fearless only when he realised that he alone was there and all others were not different from him.

Result of Self-knowledge: The knowledge of Vedānta makes me truly fearless and happy. It puts an end to all my suffering. Worldly joys are always conditioned by many external and internal factors. Sometime the cake is too sweet and sometime the stomach is not fine. But the Self is of the nature of unconditioned

Bliss. It is not that the Self/Truth has happiness, but the Self is Happiness.

Liberation from sorrow and gain of Bliss is our birth right. What is needed is a pure, concentrated and subtle mind, a mind that is discriminative, has dispassion and a longing for Truth.

Vedānta is priceless: Vedānta is the knowledge of the Truth and the valid means that reveals the Truth. This knowledge is priceless and cannot be bought or sold. It is acquired through grace – the grace of God and the Guru. A priest in his sermon said, 'Knowledge is free like water ...' When at the end of the sermon, a collection plate was passed around, one man said, "Father, you just said that knowledge was free like water!" The priest said, "Water is free, but money is required to lay the pipelines." Money is needed to print books, organise talks and the infrastructure to propagate the knowledge. Money cannot buy the knowledge, but the facilities that facilitate the gain of knowledge.

Relative differences, absolute oneness: We have so far discussed about the relative and the absolute relationship of the individual, the world and God and how to apply this knowledge in life. Let us summarise.

At the relative plane, the individual is the experiencer of the world and the world is experienced. The individual identified to the body-mind-intellect is part of God. God is the whole. God is the Creator, the material and the sentient cause of the world which includes time, space, objects (things and beings) with names, forms and qualities. God is omniscient, omnipotent, the ruler who presides over all actions and bestows results of all actions. He is just and compassionate and the friend of all. The world is an appearance that is born from, exists in and merges into God. However at the absolute plane, the individual, world and God are one – the one infinite, Existence-Consciousness-Bliss. This one Truth alone appears as these three entities.

So far logic (yukti) and examples from life and experience of Realised Masters (anubhūti) were narrated to authenticate the Truth. Now the Upaniṣads (śrutis) are quoted to validate the knowledge.

आनन्दं ब्रह्मणो विद्वान्न बिभेति कुतश्चन ।
ब्रह्मविच्चापि भवति ब्रह्मैव न हि संशयः ॥ २६ ॥

ānandaṁ brahmaṇo vidvān-na bibheti kutaścana,
brahmaviccāpi bhavati brahmaiva na hi saṁśayaḥ. (26)

आनन्दम् – bliss; ब्रह्मणः – of Brahman; विद्वान् – the knower; न – does not; बिभेति – fear; कुतश्चन – of anyone or anything; ब्रह्मवित् – the knower of Brahman; च अपि – also; भवति – becomes; ब्रह्म – Brahman; एव – itself; न – no; हि – definitely; संशयः – doubt

26. 'The knower of bliss of Brahman is not afraid of anyone or anything'. 'Knower of Brahman becomes Brahman alone'. There is no doubt about it.

The Assertion of the Upaniṣads: It is only the wrong notion that the world is different from me that causes fear. The *Taittirīya Upaniṣad* reaffirms twice that the one who knows the Truth has no fear.[1] Some are fearless despite a cause for fear. The Realised Master is fearless because there is no cause for fear.

Absolute Bliss: The Truth is of the nature of absolute Bliss. The joy of this world has various degrees. When the husband is told that his wife is expecting, he feels happy (priya). On receiving the news of the child's birth, he is overjoyed (moda) and when he sees and hugs his child, he is in ecstasy (pramoda). The Truth is not experienced in degrees, but as pure homogenous Bliss. All joys of the world are understood to be the expressions of this Bliss alone similar to the zero watt, hundred watt and a thousand watt bulb that manifest the same electricity in degrees of brightness of light.

Knower becomes the known: The knower always remains different from the known. The child who sees the monkey, does not become one, even if he acts like one. The only exception is Self-knowledge.

---

[1] *ānandaṁ brahmaṇo vidvān, na bibheti kutaścaneti*

– *Taittirīya Upaniṣad*-2.9

ānando brahmaṇo vidvān, na bibheti kadācaneti

– *Taittirīya Upaniṣad*-2.4

Herein the one who knows the Truth/Self, becomes the Truth/Self, just as the dreamer awakens to become the waker. It is not that he becomes the Truth, he realises that he is the Truth.

Also the Truth cannot be known in degrees. The infinite cannot be known in finite parts or stages. One cannot become 50% realised. The infinite Truth has to be realised as 'I am the infinite Truth'. Anything other than this is not Realisation. The knower of the Truth is verily the Truth.

Doubtlessly True: There is always a doubt whether we will become rich, or if we are rich whether we will remain so, to that extent. However there is no doubt that I am the infinite Truth. This knowledge is never lost whatever be the circumstances that the Realised Master faces thereafter. There is no doubt that the Realised Master will always remain so.

It seems difficult for the knowledge to sink in and to live it. How should we do so?

एवं वेदान्तज्ञानस्य नित्यमभ्यासयोगतः ।
श्रेयः परमवाप्नोति सर्वभावेन साधकः ॥ २७ ॥

evaṁ vedānta-jñānasya nityam-abhyāsa-yogataḥ,
śreyaḥ param-avāpnoti sarvabhāvena sādhakaḥ. (27)

एवम् – thus (as explained); वेदान्तज्ञानस्य – of this knowledge of Upaniṣads; नित्यम्-अभ्यास-योगतः – by constant reflection and practice; श्रेयः – good; परम् – supreme; अवाप्नोति – attains; सर्वभावेन – by wholehearted; साधकः – seeker

27. Thus through wholehearted constant reflection and practice of this knowledge of Vedānta, a seeker attains the supreme Good.

Practise to perfection: Initially when we read or hear of this knowledge, it seems unbelievable. 'How can I be infinite?' As we listen often, reflect and understand, we appreciate the knowledge, but it seems impossible to live it.

A beggar is overnight crowned the king. He would naturally find it difficult to think of himself as the king. He may act like one, but his thinking may remain beggarly. He will need to open his mind to his new identity and constantly ascertain it to be able to truly live like a king. Old habits die hard. In Indian politics, some members of Parliament who have been in the opposition for long, continue to voice strong protests in Parliament and stage walkouts even when they are part of the ruling party. They forget that they are not sitting in the opposition anymore.

The mind is unable to abide in the knowledge because of past habits, distractions and weaknesses. The solution is constant and wholehearted practice. Śrī Ramana Maharshi says, 'Reflect again and again to strengthen the knowledge, as the mind is weak and does not abide in the Truth.'[1]

Nature of practice: Practice of Vedānta does not mean any physical action like prāṇāyāma. It is to remind ourselves time and again and live a conscious and alert life with the vision of Vedānta.

[1] *bhūyo vicāro matidurbalatvam – Saddarśana*-34

Each time you feel helpless – remind yourself, I am infinite. When you feel sad, assert 'I am Bliss Absolute ...' Spiritual practices like ritualistic worship (pūjā), japa (repetition of God's name or a mantra) will help us to purify the mind. Listening to the scriptures (śravaṇa), reflection on the scriptures (manana) and meditation or contemplation on the knowledge (nididhyāsana) will strengthen the knowledge. A pure, concentrated and subtle mind easily abides in the Truth. We naturally live in the knowledge we abide in and therefore, living Vedānta becomes easy and joyous.

Supreme good: Self-knowledge leads to one's absolute good (paraṁ śreyas). Usually what is good for one, may not be good for another. Sweets may be fine for someone, but may not for one with diabetes. But Self-knowledge is good for all, for all times.

In the gain of one, there might be the loss to another. My company profits by capturing the market at the loss to my competitor. But in the attainment of the Truth, there is only the gain of absolute Bliss. The only loss is the loss of ignorance and ignorance born wrong notions. With the realisation that the Self in me is the Self of all, the Realised Master serves all through his life, works and teachings. His very presence is a blessing to all.

The text ends with a verse of dedication.

श्रीरामचन्द्रस्य कृपाप्रसादाद्वेदान्तचिन्तनपराकृतिर्या ।
समर्पये तां पदारविन्दयोर्भूयात्प्रसन्नः श्रीरामोगुरुश्च ॥ २८ ॥

śrīrāmacandrasya kṛpāprasādād-vedānta-cintana-
parākṛtir-yā,
samarpaye tāṁ padāravindayor-bhūyāt-prasannaḥ
śrīrāmo-guruśca. (28)

श्रीरामचन्द्रस्य – Lord Śrī Rāma's; कृपाप्रसादात् – by the grace and blessings; वेदान्तचिन्तन – *Vedānta Cintanam;* पराकृतिः – composition on the Supreme Truth(?); या – which (is); समर्पये – I dedicate; ताम् – that (composition); पदारविन्दयोः – to His Lotus Feet; भूयात् – may (they) be; प्रसन्नः – pleased; श्रीरामः – Śrī Rāma; च – and; गुरुः – Guru

28. This composition Vedānta Cintanam is the result of Lord Śrī Rāma's grace and blessings. I dedicate it to His lotus feet. May Śrī Rāma and my Guru be pleased with it.

Grace: God is the creator, sustainer and destroyer of all. He alone accomplishes everything. It is He who inspired this composition and gave me an opportunity to reflect on Vedānta. It is His will that I speak on it and His grace that the commentary is written and printed.

Offering: God alone deserves to be offered what is His.[1] Whatever I do with my body, speech, senses, mind, intellect and nature, I offer to the Supreme Lord.[2] That is Bhāgavata Dharma.

Prayer: May Lord Śrī Rāma and Gurudev be pleased with my humble offering. That is my only wish and my sincere prayer.

May all be happy.

Om tat sat śrī rāmārpaṇam astu

---

[1] *terā tujhako arpaṇa kyā lāge merā*

[2] *kāyena vācā manasaindriyairvā buddhyātmanā vā prakṛteḥ svabhāvāt, karomi yadyat sakalaṁ parasmai nārāyaṇāyeti samarpayāmi*

श्रीरामाय नमस्तुभ्यं कृपया तव शक्यते ।
सुखेनाभ्यसितुं लब्धं ज्ञानं दैनिकजीवने ॥ १ ॥

śrīrāmāya namastubhyaṁ kṛpayā tava śakyate,
sukhenābhyasituṁ labdhaṁ jñānaṁ dainika-jīvane. (1)

वेदान्तदर्शनं शुद्धं प्रत्यक्षानुभवं परम् ।
सर्वदा येऽनुतिष्ठन्ति प्राप्यते तैर्ध्रुवं पदम् ॥ २ ॥

vedānta-darśanaṁ śuddhaṁ pratyakṣānubhavaṁ param,
sarvadā ye'nutiṣṭhanti prāpyate tair-dhruvaṁ padam. (2)

नाहङ्कारो मनोबुद्धिर्देहो नाहं कदाचन ।
इति वेदान्तवाक्यस्य भावश्चिन्त्यः पुनः पुनः ॥ ३ ॥

nāhaṅkāro mano-buddhir-deho nāhaṁ kadācana,
iti vedānta-vākyasya bhāvaścintyaḥ punaḥ punaḥ. (3)

तेषामात्मत्वमात्रं हि निरस्तमिह नास्तिता ।
योजनीयाश्च तस्मात्ते व्यवहारे विवेकतः ॥ ४ ॥

teṣām-ātmatva-mātraṁ hi nirastam-iha nāstitā,
yojanīyāśca tasmāt-te vyavahāre vivekataḥ. (4)

नरदेहः पुण्यप्राप्तः सर्वभूतहिते सदा।
निःश्रेयसि च योक्तव्यः सर्वेशे चातिप्रेमतः॥ ५॥

nara-dehaḥ puṇya-prāptaḥ sarvabhūta-hite sadā,
niḥśreyasi ca yoktavyaḥ sarveśe cātiprematah. (5)

अनिष्टमिष्टं मिश्रं च फलं प्राप्नोति मानवः।
कृतकर्मानुसारेण समत्वं तेषु धारयेत्॥ ६॥

aniṣṭam-iṣṭaṁ miśraṁ ca phalaṁ prāpnoti mānavaḥ,
kṛta-karmānusāreṇa samatvaṁ teṣu dhārayet. (6)

यस्मादृते न किञ्चन क्रियते कर्म मानवैः।
तन्मनः कल्पनारूपं योज्यतां सावधानतः॥ ७॥

yasmād-ṛte na kiñcana kriyate karma mānavaiḥ,
tanmanaḥ kalpanā-rūpaṁ yojyatāṁ sāvadhānataḥ. (7)

विषयासक्तिरूपेण मनो बन्धनकारकम्।
ईश्वरार्पितरूपेण तन्मनो मुक्तिसाधकम्॥ ८॥

viṣayāsakti-rūpeṇa mano bandhana-kārakam,
īśvarārpita-rūpeṇa tanmano mukti-sādhakam. (8)

तस्मात्सदा हि ध्यातव्यं साधकेन प्रयत्नतः।
मनो मे शिवसङ्कल्पमस्तु ते कृपया प्रभो॥ ९॥

tasmāt-sadā hi dhyātavyaṁ sādhakena prayatnataḥ,
mano me śiva-saṅkalpam-astu te kṛpayā prabho. (9)

बुद्धिं तु सारथिं विद्धि या नयेद्रथजीवनम् ।
कार्याकार्यविवेकेन मनुष्यस्य दिने दिने ॥ १० ॥

buddhiṁ tu sārathiṁ viddhi yā nayed-ratha-jīvanam,
kāryākārya-vivekena manuṣyasya dine dine. (10)

यद्विषये प्रमाणं यज्जानीयात् तत्प्रमाणतः ।
स्वरूपं निश्चितं तस्य कर्म कुर्यान्नरस्ततः ॥ ११ ॥

yadviṣaye pramāṇaṁ yajjānīyāt tatpramāṇataḥ,
svarūpaṁ niścitaṁ tasya karma kuryānnarastataḥ. (11)

व्यवहारे चिकित्सादिशास्त्राणि विविधानि स्युः ।
उपयोगं नरस्तेषां यथा कुर्यात्परिस्थितिः ॥ १२ ॥

vyavahāre cikitsādi-śāstrāṇi vividhāni syuḥ,
upayogaṁ naras-teṣāṁ yathā kuryāt-paristhitiḥ. (12)

श्रुतिः स्मृतिश्च धर्मादौ वेदान्तो ब्रह्मदर्शने ।
प्रमाणं विद्यते साक्षात् किमन्येन प्रयोजनम् ॥ १३ ॥

śrutiḥ smṛtiśca dharmādau vedānto brahma-darśane,
pramāṇaṁ vidyate sākṣāt kim-anyena prayojanam. (13)

अहङ्कारः स विज्ञेयस्तादात्म्येन हि जायते ।
देहादिभिर्गुणैः साकं यो विभाति तथा तथा ॥ १४ ॥

ahaṅkāraḥ sa vijñeyas-tādātmyena hi jāyate,
dehādibhir-guṇaiḥ sākaṁ yo vibhāti tathā tathā. (14)

अहङ्कारस्तु द्विविधो बन्धरूपश्च मुक्तिदः ।
पूज्यभावश्चात्मनीह कर्ता भोक्ता स बन्धकः ॥ १५ ॥

ahaṅkārastu dvividho bandha-rūpaśca muktidaḥ,
pūjya-bhāvaścātmanīha kartā bhoktā sa bandhakaḥ. (15)

ईश्वरस्यैव दासोऽहं न परेषां कदाचन ।
मतिरित्थं मोचयति कामनाकर्मबन्धनात् ॥ १६ ॥

īśvarasyaiva dāso'haṁ na pareṣāṁ kadācana,
matir-itthaṁ mocayati kāmanā-karma-bandhanāt. (16)

देहादिभ्यः उपाधिभ्यः परात्मा भिन्न एव सः ।
सच्चिदानन्दरूपोऽयं ब्रह्मरूपः सनातनः ॥ १७ ॥

dehādibhyaḥ upādhibhyaḥ parātmā bhinna eva saḥ,
saccidānanda-rūpo'yaṁ brahma-rūpaḥ sanātanaḥ. (17)

ज्ञानेनैतेन शास्त्रस्य जगत्यस्मिंश्च सर्वदा ।
आनन्दस्वामिनः सन्तु लोका नानन्दयाचकाः ॥ १८ ॥

jñānenaitena śāstrasya jagatyasmiṁśca sarvadā,
ānanda-svāminaḥ santu lokā nānanda-yācakāḥ. (18)

ईश्वरः सर्वभूतानां सर्वदा हृदि वर्तते ।
तदन्तर्यामिरूपेण सर्वभूतसुहृत्तया ॥ १९ ॥

īśvaraḥ sarvabhūtānāṁ sarvadā hṛdi vartate,
tad-antaryāmi-rūpeṇa sarvabhūta-suhṛttayā. (19)

समोऽयं सर्वभूतेषु निष्पक्षो जलमेघवत् ।
तमेव शरणं गत्वा शान्तिमाप्नोति मानवः ॥ २० ॥

samo'yaṁ sarvabhūteṣu niṣpakṣo jala-meghavat,
tameva śaraṇaṁ gatvā śāntim-āpnoti mānavaḥ. (20)

ईश्वरेच्छातिरिक्ता मे मा भूयात्कामना कदा ।
एषा मतिर्हि भक्तस्य शरणागतिरिष्यते ॥ २१ ॥

īśvarecchātiriktā me mā bhūyāt-kāmanā kadā,
eṣā matir-hi bhaktasya śaraṇāgatir-iṣyate. (21)

ब्रह्मणः सर्वभूतानि प्रतिभान्ति स्थितानि च ।
तस्मिन्नेव लयं यान्ति सर्ववेदान्तनिश्चयः ॥ २२ ॥

brahmaṇaḥ sarvabhūtāni pratibhānti sthitāni ca,
tasminneva layaṁ yānti sarvavedānta-niścayaḥ. (22)

आत्मरूपेण तद्ब्रह्म सर्वभूतहृदि स्थितम् ।
गूढ भावोऽस्य शास्त्रस्य ज्ञातव्यश्च मुमुक्षुभिः ॥२३ ॥

ātma-rūpeṇa tadbrahma sarvabhūta-hṛdi sthitam,
gūḍha bhāvo'sya śāstrasya jñātavyaśca mumukṣubhiḥ. (23)

इदं जगद्वस्तुतश्च ब्रह्मभिन्नं न सिध्यति ।
तथैव चात्मभिन्नं वा ब्रह्मात्मैक्यप्रबोधनात् ॥ २४ ॥

idaṁ jagadvastutaśca brahma-bhinnaṁ na sidhyati,
tathaiva cātma-bhinnaṁ vā brahmātmaikya-
prabodhanāt. (24)